HEALING FROM THE INSIDE OUT

AN INFORMATIONAL WORKBOOK

Becoming Your Authentic Self While Navigating
Compassion Fatigue and/or Secondary Traumatic Stress

DEB ALVERSON, M.Ed.

Book Cover and Interior Formatting by 100Covers.com

Website: www.professionaldevelopmentmanagement.org
Email: healingfromtheinsideout63@gmail.com

ISBN – Paper back: 979-8-89121-543-6
ISBN – Epub/Ebook: 979-8-89121-544-3
First Edition: September 2023

TABLE OF CONTENTS

DEDICATION

I am dedicating this book to my husband, *Jim*. He has been by my side my entire career, supporting me through my trials, my many mood swings, and my tears, while I was trying to understand "what is wrong with me." Over the many years, I've researched what I now know as Compassion Fatigue and Secondary Traumatic Stress; I did not always put him first, yet he kept encouraging me. One day he told me, "You're so passionate about this topic, write a book." So, with love in my heart and gratefulness to him… Jim, I love you.

PREFACE

I first became interested in STS when, while living in Utah, one of my students came and told me about witnessing the murder of someone in his family by another member. By then, I had been a certified counselor for approximately eight years. I have helped thousands of school-aged children navigate traumas, life experiences, and other mental health issues. I thought I could always go home at the end of my working day and put work aside for the evening. Yes, I thought about some of my students off and on, especially those living in what I believed was a hostile environment. I always thought I felt for them simply because I cared. While that was and still is true, it was not until this young man told me about what he witnessed six years before this date that what I now know as Secondary Traumatic Stress (STS) symptoms became blatantly apparent.

I did not understand what was happening. I did not put 2+2 together in my mind. I could not sleep, I was irritable, and I began feeling less empathy for my students who came to me with lesser problems, thinking at least they did not go through what so and so went through. I had no patience when previously it would seem like nothing bothered me. I started thinking about my childhood, which had its challenges and trauma, and I lost interest in doing the things that matter most to me. I didn't understand what was happening to me; however, I knew I needed to figure it out quickly.

I started doing what most intelligent people do; I googled my symptoms (lol). Lots of different things came up; depression, anxiety, burnout at work, and then the one term that came to my attention piqued my curiosity, Compassion Fatigue. I then tried googling everything I could find about compassion fatigue. Frankly, there wasn't much out there. Other words popped up in my searches, like Secondary Traumatic Stress and Vicarious Trauma; however, while explaining what it is, they did not provide the details of STS or what to do about it. I knew other people must suffer from this if I was experiencing this. At that point, I researched this topic, and by doing so, I cured myself of STS, and since then, I have helped numerous others cure themselves as well.

If you are a professional working in any service-oriented industry, such as a firefighter, a police officer, a nurse, a teacher, an EMS worker, a social worker, or a first responder.; this workbook is for you. You, too, may experience symptoms of something you do not quite understand. You may think, why is such-and-such affecting me so much? Suppose you know and care about someone who may experience this. There is hope because you can live your best life by healing from the inside out and becoming authentic while navigating Compassion Fatigue or Secondary Traumatic Stress (STS).

INTRODUCTION

You have been on your altruistic journey for most, if not your entire life. You will do anything for anyone. Yes, you may get paid a salary for what you do; however, you would also do it just because you are you. Along this expedition called life, humans encounter STS socially, cognitively, emotionally, physically, and spiritually. Welcome to the beginning of your trek, "healing from the inside out, finding authenticity while navigating compassion fatigue or secondary traumatic stress or STS."

If you accept it, your mission will encompass two parts of your journey. Part I of this workbook includes five stops along your trek toward "healing from the inside out." Part II will be your action guide. This is where you will explore putting everything you have learned into action. You will find your "authenticity while navigating compassion fatigue and/or secondary traumatic stress (STS)."

At the first stop, your experience will include an overview of compassion fatigue and secondary traumatic stress (STS). Throughout this workbook, we will interchangeably use the letters "STS" to mean compassion fatigue or secondary traumatic stress. Your second stop will navigate through STS risk factors or what risk factors put someone in your line of work at a higher possibility of developing STS. Your exploration continues at stop three, where you will assess yourself for STS. You will then travel to stop four, exploring how STS affects you, and finally, arrive at stop five – the self-care crossing. This is where you will develop your individualized self-care plan, designed specifically by you and for you.

After completing Part I, you will continue to Part II of your voyage. Throughout Part II, you will take what you have learned on your journey and put them into action. Some of these adventures include:

- Inspiration to Living out your Dreams.

- Permitting yourself to do what is best for you.

- Navigating toward your best life ever.

- Building your self-esteem and self-concept.

- Healing from the inside out.

- Healed from the inside out.

- Being your authentic self.

- Love who you are.

So, if you are ready, climb aboard and join the countless other individuals like yourself who have healed from the inside out and found their authenticity while navigating Compassion Fatigue and/or Secondary Traumatic Stress.

PART I

BEGINNING THE JOURNEY

HEALING FROM THE
INSIDE OUT...
...AND SO IT BEGINS

OVERVIEW OF
SECONDARY TRAUMATIC STRESS (STS)

Stop 1 – What is Secondary Traumatic Stress?

Secondary Traumatic Stress (STS) is a condition that occurs when individuals are exposed to trauma through someone else's experiences. It is a type of trauma that affects those who work with trauma survivors, such as first responders, healthcare professionals, and mental health professionals, to name a few. STS can also occur among family members and friends of trauma survivors. It's crucial to remember that Secondary Traumatic Stress (STS) is not a result of personal flaws or shortcomings but a by-product of our compassionate and caring roles in service professions. Our daily efforts to support individuals, many of whom are facing trying circumstances, can lead to STS. Recognizing the signs and symptoms of STS, and learning how to manage it, is a crucial aspect of being a well-rounded human being. Before arriving at stop two, we hope you will differentiate between trauma and stress, understand compassion fatigue and secondary traumatic stress, and know the most common signs of STS.

The Substance Abuse and Mental Health Services Administration (SAMHSA) defines trauma as "the aftermath of a singular event or a series of events that an individual perceives as physically or emotionally damaging or life-threatening" (SAMHSA, n.d.). This can negatively impact a person's physical, emotional, social, mental, and spiritual health and overall functioning. Trauma may be considered a sudden shock to the system, but what about stress? Stress is often intertwined with trauma and can contribute to it. Secondary Traumatic Stress (STS) is the term used to describe this phenomenon; still, in this context, we are using "stress" to refer to the typical daily stressors that most people face, such as conflicts with coworkers, traffic delays, being late, or arguments with a partner or child (SAMSHA, n.d.). While these stressors can frustrate and even be distressing, they rarely reach the level of trauma. Mental health professionals often categorize traumatic reactions to negative experiences into four main types. Let's examine these categories.

- **Acute** trauma results from limited-duration incidents, such as car accidents, single acts of violence, or exposure to natural or human-made disasters.

- **Chronic** trauma stems from repeated experiences, such as continuous exposure to violence in the community or medical traumas like chronic illness or painful medical procedures.

- **Complex** trauma begins early and continues over time within the caregiving environment, such as repeated incidents of neglect, physical abuse, or other harmful experiences.

- **Historical** trauma stems from accumulating physical, psychological, and social wounds over a person's lifespan and across generations. Historical trauma occurs because of traumatic events that a group has experienced. For instance, this kind of trauma is straightforward in communities like Native Americans and Holocaust survivors.

These four categories provide a general understanding; however, trauma can also be differentiated in other ways. It can be categorized as violent or non-violent, human-caused, natural, physical, or psychological, affecting individuals or communities. Some types of traumas fall easily within these categories and are readily identifiable. For instance, it is widely understood that earthquakes and military conflicts can cause trauma for those impacted. However, trauma can also be more subtle. For example, renewal efforts in a neighborhood leading to increased housing costs can be traumatic for residents forced to move away from their homes. Trauma can encompass multiple categories and not be confined to just one.

Why does giving a label or name to trauma matter? It becomes easier to understand and process one's experiences by providing a name to the trauma. This allows for the externalization of these traumatic experiences, recognition of related symptoms, and a reduction in feeling defined by them. Naming the trauma can help take control and prepare oneself to cope with the traumatic stress more healthily. Traumatic events can impact individuals in different ways. They can be directly experienced, observed while happening to others, learned about when it affects someone close such as a relative, friend, or recipient, or repeated exposure to the traumatic details through various sources.

During this expedition, we will emphasize the final mode of exposure. This is commonly referred to as compassion fatigue, secondary trauma, or as per SAMHSA's definition, "emotional distress that arises from hearing or witnessing firsthand the traumatic experiences of others" (SAMHSA, n.d.). A significant portion of our understanding of STS stems from the experiences of individuals in helping professions, such as First Responders. While your job may not immediately appear at risk of STS, working with groups such as students, children, the elderly, the ill, and those in need can present many opportunities for developing compassion fatigue or secondary trauma. For this mission, students, clients, patients, the public, and anyone you serve will be titled recipient, beneficiary, or individual. Individuals who receive support from us may have gone through one or multiple traumas in the past or may be currently facing traumatic experiences. A national study shows that 60% of people in the United States have gone through trauma in the past 12 months (*Children's Exposure to Violence, n.d.*). When the recipients we serve exhibit challenging behavior to manage, it is essential to remember that they may struggle with untreated post-traumatic stress. A helpful approach is considering their experiences and what they may have witnessed. You may recall traumatic events that the recipients have shared with you or overheard them discussing, which have impacted you or that you find complicated to forget. The following self-reflection exercise can reflect on these experiences.

Self-Reflection Exercise

Reflect on your experiences hearing about your recipients' trauma by answering the following questions below:

Have any of your recipients' shared details of traumatic events in their lives with you? If so, describe the events shared with you.

Have you overheard recipients discussing such events? These include physical, emotional, or sexual abuse, community violence, victimization, abandonment or neglect, and other traumatic events. Describe the events you have overheard.

How did hearing about these experiences affect you?

It is essential to remember perception is everything with secondary trauma. Your response to hearing about or seeing traumatic occurrences may differ from someone else's. What matters is how the event affects you because of hearing about or seeing it. You can read some examples of real people who have experienced STS below, in their own words:

Experience of Robert R - Adolescent Social Worker

"The secondary trauma that has happened to me has been in situations where I have a child share like, you know, someone died of cancer or a child telling me that, you know, when he was four years old or five, he was walking home, and he saw a body in the river with the throat slashed, or I'm hearing about this kid who told me just a few days ago they got a gun pulled on him and his little sister as they were walking home from school. How do I process that when I'm at work and stay strong for the kids I counsel? I feel guilty because I feel safe in my life, and I go home in my car, where I feel safe. Still, I'm sending what I call my babies back into their unsafe (real or perceptually) outside of therapy life, and it's hard not to, you know, every night, wonder did they make it home safely."

Experience of Georgia P. - EMS Worker

"When I was on the job and started feeling symptoms of STS, I was exhausted. I would isolate, like when it was the worst, in one stop where I saved an individual in cardiac arrest but still thought about them, knowing they didn't have much support at home. It affected my relationships outside work and with my friends or family when we got together. They would talk about problems they had at work like it was so annoying the copy machine didn't work; how can you even know what real problems at work are like? I wasn't very empathetic, and I wasn't interested in hearing about stuff like that because it became like the people just took up so much space in my head because I wasn't doing any self-care things I could have done. It just became so big there wasn't room in my life for anything else."

Experience of Lisa B. - Police Officer

"Patrolling in a low-income neighborhood, I deal with many stressors and traumatic events that our civilians deal with. You know, the loss of a parent in another country or gang violence in those types of things, and so, if you truly have a good relationship with the people in the neighborhood, you patrol, you take that on. So a lot of time as a police officer, I'm constantly dealing with the trauma that the residents are dealing with. Because I have many civilians to deal with, I have multiple stories being weighed upon me on top of whatever I'm dealing with personally. It can be very stressful and tough; it's tough sometimes if you don't learn to do self-care. I take on their traumas without even realizing it."

Which individual's story do you relate to the most? Have you had experiences like the ones described? If so, how have they been similar? How have they differed?

Vicarious traumatization is a different phrase that is occasionally used synonymously with STS. The experience of traumatic stress because of hearing about or seeing parts of the terrible experiences of others is the common thread that unites all the terminology used to define STS. Burnout in the workplace is another term you may be familiar with. This phrase describes the exhaustion and unhappiness from a challenging work environment. Despite sharing symptoms of STS, such as physical and emotional tiredness, professional burnout differs from STS in one crucial way; it does not include exposure to hearing about other recipients' painful experiences. It can frequently be treated by altering one's working environment. There are four frequent responses to hearing about or seeing parts of someone else's traumatic experience, although everyone responds to STS differently.

- **Intrusive thoughts or re-experiencing the incident.** This may manifest as nightmares or flashbacks to the recipient's experience. For instance, you might discover that hearing about your beneficiaries' experiences keeps playing back in your head.

- **You are feeling on edge and awaiting something terrible to happen.** You may find it difficult to concentrate or feel angrier or more irritable than usual. You can have feelings of anxiety, panic, or being easily startled. This is sometimes referred to as arousal. Hypervigilance is a sense associated with arousal. This is where you constantly look around you for potential threats.

- **Avoidance.** This may involve avoiding certain situations, people, or sensations that make you think of what happened to your recipient. Some people might isolate themselves socially, cease taking care of themselves, or stop listening to recipients out of concern for hearing about further painful occurrences.

- **Adverse shifts in your thoughts or emotions.** You can find it challenging to focus, feel disoriented, feel guilty, or be unhappy about what happened to your recipient. You may have a more pessimistic outlook on the world or yourself than usual. You might experience guilt, helplessness, rage, or cynicism. You can find it difficult to fall asleep, feel distant from others, or lose your sensitivity to violent behavior. You might experience chronic fatigue, decreased creativity, and unusually high levels of irritability.

Not everyone will experience all these symptoms, and the severity with which they manifest varies. Let's look at several service providers who are afflicted with STS. We will work together to identify the symptoms after reading the scenarios.

- Because of her personable, compassionate demeanor, Janice, a CPS Caseworker, is well-liked by coworkers and her clients. She has a great work ethic. She serves a neighborhood with unusually high violence rates, and her clients frequently confide in her about distressing events. She has recently called in sick to work because of extreme exhaustion, napping the entire day away. She is so overcome with remorse over her subpar work performance that she has quit dining in the staff lounge to prevent her coworkers from asking her about her absences. Outside work, she is slow to respond to calls and texts, hesitant to go out with friends, and prefers to stay home and watch TV.

What are the STS symptoms Janice is feeling?

- Fatigue

- Anger

- Disturbed Sleep Patterns

- Guilt

- Frustration

- Hypervigilance

While many of these are STS symptoms, Janice is specifically experiencing guilt, disturbed sleep patterns, and fatigue. She feels this way because she cannot fulfill her commitments at work. Her consumers like and trust her; therefore, they open up to her about many distressing details regarding tragic incidents. Daily exposure to these kinds of stories has impacted her severely.

- Third-grade teacher Tyanna is getting ready for class when one of her pupils enters, sobbing and trembling. Tyanna ultimately learns that she was meant to be driven to school by her elder brother, but he was running late and abandoned her a block from campus. An unknown male tried to entice her into his car as he drove beside her. A childhood memory of Tyanna's close friend being abducted and killed suddenly floods her mind. Throughout the day, Tyanna frequently drifts off during parent-teacher conferences and in the middle of lessons. In the following weeks, she keeps playing over her pupils' ordeal in her thoughts and feels as if she is examining her terror and anguish after her buddy went missing and then passed away again. She becomes agitated around her relatives at home. Her daily attendance at work is depleting all her energy.

What are the STS symptoms Tyanna is feeling?

- Cynicism

- Intrusive Thoughts

- Irritability

- Lack of Energy

- Loss of Creativity

- Guilt

Tyanna's reaction to learning about her student's terrifying event was unfavorable. She keeps thinking about her own painful experience from childhood and revisiting the narrative her student told her. She is having intrusive thoughts. She has no energy to accomplish much more than get to work every day, which makes her irritated with her family.

These illustrations show how working with traumatized individuals can put us at a greater risk for STS. It makes sense that we would have emotions after hearing about the traumatic experiences our recipients have shared with us, perhaps repeatedly. However, the good news is STS can be overcome since it is a typical response to an unusual circumstance. We may support a recipient without sacrificing our personal or professional well-being, and realizing the symptoms of STS is a crucial first step in safeguarding our mental health.

NAVIGATING THROUGH STS RISK FACTORS

Stop 2 – Examining the Risk Factors

Secondary traumatic stress, or STS, and its accompanying symptoms, including nightmares, difficulty concentrating, avoidance of places or objects, and depressive changes in mood, may affect anyone in any helping profession, as we discovered while at stop one. We will expand on what we learned at stop one by examining the risk factors that put you at a higher risk of getting STS. Exposure to STS can be prevalent, with a national average of roughly 60% (*Children's Exposure to Violence, n.d.*)., as was stated during our time at stop one.

Because you are uniquely positioned to build relationships of trust with receivers, the number of people in any helping or serving profession is more significant. Recipients turn to us for help or consolation. It is not always the case that each time they visit us or have an event that will lead to the development of STS, but over time; it can significantly raise your chances of having at least some STS symptoms. Understanding the risk factors unique to your profession and you are crucial. The three risk factors discussed in this section are the people you serve, your personality, and your workplace. After completing this section of the mission, you will identify the specific risk factors applicable to your place of employment and the characteristics of your personality that could make you more susceptible to STS.

EMS personnel, teachers, healthcare professionals, police officers, and firefighters, for instance, frequently have STS symptoms resulting from their line of work. Your work involves interacting with a population that, like all helping and service-oriented professions, may handle acute or chronic trauma, including domestic violence, serious illness, unsafe living conditions, as well as the kinds of losses that almost all of us experience, like the natural death of a family member or pet. As previously mentioned, STS happens because of hearing about or seeing parts of another person's experiences. Our receivers occasionally confide in us about their experiences. On other occasions, we learn about their circumstances via a coworker, another person, a bystander, a family member, a witness, etc. Regardless of the source, we risk getting STS if we cannot move past these experiences, absorb them, and recognize what we can and cannot do to support our recipients.

Our STS risk levels increase proportionally to the recipient populations we serve when we operate in a setting where beneficiaries routinely experience high rates of trauma. As part of your duties, you might learn about or see beneficiaries being exploited, harassed, threatened, or even subjected to domestic violence or other forms of abuse. People who live in high-poverty areas, both urban and rural, people who are food insecure, people who live in high-crime areas, etc., are examples of recipient populations who may suffer trauma at levels higher than typical. These people are more likely to have multiple exposures to trauma, violence, and severe stress. For instance, 40 percent of 11-year-old children in one urban community said they had witnessed knife or gun violence the previous year (*Children's Exposure to Violence, n.d.*). Recipients in these extremely low-income areas are more likely to participate in gang and inter-community violence. You might run into other beneficiary demographics, such as individuals who are homeless. The likelihood of these encountering the juvenile justice and child welfare systems may be higher. Children whose parents suffer from alcohol or drug addiction are another group at risk of high levels of trauma. You are likely to work with LGBTQ+ kids and adults who, compared to their straight peers, encounter higher rates of bullying, harassment, sexual assault, and rejection from family members. These individuals are also at risk of trauma. Other people at risk for trauma include undocumented immigrants or children living in neighborhoods with a high fear of losing parents or other family members because of deportation. These people are likely to be the clients you work with.

It is also important to mention the recipients who have experienced a singular crisis. This might be a terrorist assault or a natural disaster like a hurricane or earthquake. A school shooting or bombing, a member of the community committing suicide, or a crime committed within the community are examples of events that could directly affect society as a whole or a portion of one. Even though these incidents are one-time rather than recurring, they may have profound consequences on the recipient's mental health and indirectly lead to the development of STS. Consider for a moment which of these groups you work with and note it below.

Our knowledge of the signs and causes of STS and our personal trauma history plays a significant role in the STS equation. Our risk factors for STS also depend on our innate and learned capacity to handle stress and how much we can relate to the plight of our recipients. Serving those who have gone through emotionally trying or physically traumatic experiences can bring back memories of our prior traumas, which can then cause an emotional or even visceral reaction. This is especially true if we have not fully recovered from these traumatic occurrences. We behave as though the recipient's feelings and experiences are our own. We may be perplexed or even scared when we experience these reactions, wondering,

"Where did these strong emotional and bodily responses originate from"? "What can I do to make them stop"?

Lack of information and training is just one reason most of us do not recognize the symptoms of STS. Rarely, if ever, do higher education programs discuss the adverse effects that service to others might have on you. Most pre-service programs barely touch on the impact of trauma, much less the idea of STS. You may have heard or seen the phrase referenced at a professional development program among peers and colleagues or perhaps stumbled across a reference in a journal paper. Whatever exposure you may have had to the idea before starting this journey, it probably wasn't enough to enable you to identify your own STS symptoms, manage them, and prevent future occurrences. How well you handle stress and how robust you are, affect your risk of getting STS.

Resilience is the capacity to recover or move forward after adversity (Feldman, 2020). Although some people are more resilient by nature than others, practically everyone can benefit from adopting resilience-enhancing practices. Fortunately, resilience can be developed. Resilience is enhanced by practicing self-care. Taking care of oneself might be difficult, but it helps you handle stress and control your emotions. Your daily tasks demand commitment, time, and effort. You frequently put your recipients' needs above yours since you are preoccupied with them. Ironically, this may prevent you from being as present for your beneficiaries, your family, and those who need you most.

Empathy is the next personal risk factor we will discuss, and it could surprise you. You may relate to what other people are going through and understand their experiences if you have empathy. You possess this virtue in your line of work, a favorable character attribute. Maybe you chose a career in service and help because you are a compassionate person who wants to improve the lives of those you aid, and you experience empathy in the course of your work daily. It would be best if you did not cease feeling empathy as a human being, but when paired with any other elements we have mentioned, it can increase your risk of developing STS. The inability to recognize and respect one's emotional boundaries might lead to STS symptoms when we are sympathetic to the horrific experiences of our recipients. Of course, it's crucial to let our recipients know that we still care about them; but it's just as essential to do it in a way that safeguards our well-being. Which of these factors apply to you?

1. I have experienced trauma in my life.

2. I have difficulty making time for self-care.

3. Until reading this book, I knew little about STS.

4. I don't handle stress well.

5. I am an empathetic person.

6. None of these.

We may be more susceptible to STS because of several personal circumstances. We can address our risk factors when we are aware of them. An excellent first step is in reading and completing this workbook. Below, you will find examples of individuals in service professions who don't immediately recognize the beginning of STS symptoms. Read these examples and answer the questions that follow.

- Jordan, a dance teacher at a famous institution for the Performing Arts, is 39 years old. She has always had a strong passion for kids, and after having a successful career as a professional dancer, she has given back by pursuing a career as a dance teacher. Jordan has been teaching Natalie, a kid who reminds her of herself when she was younger, for the past year. Jordan has heard Natalie's feel-ings about how she feels differently and about her prior suicide attempts. Jordan never attempted suicide as a teenager; however, she battled feelings of worthlessness and rejection. These feelings are slightly lessened by the plaudits she has earned for her dancing, but Jordan has never really examined them; instead, she prefers to bury them and move on. Jordan nearly feels Natalie's anguish as if it were her own when she hears about her experiences. While traveling, preparing dinner, and even lying in bed at night, she frequently considers Natalie. She observes herself being extremely possessive of Natalie in class and getting angry with other students when they do not perform well. She struggles to concentrate on her other lessons, frequently becoming lost and thinking back on her past. Stephanie, her only close friend, has invited her out for lunch numerous times, but she always has an explanation for declining, preferring to eat alone in her car. She occasionally experiences odd anxiety that Natalie has been injured. She is convinced that Natalie won't attend class, so she feels forced to arrive early. Jordan knows something is wrong and must discuss her situation with someone.

Think about Jordan's situation and answer the following questions:

Why was Jordan thinking about Natalie so often?

What personal risk factors cause Jordan to be predisposed to STS?

Does Jordan realize she may suffer from STS?

The final risk factor to be aware of is our work environment. Any workplace can either add to or detract from our ability to function well, and our job and work systems are no exception. Working in an environment that encourages their staff to attend to self-care and provides the support to do so, acknowledges the emotional challenges of serving and supporting others, and encourages workers to practice self-care may lessen the risk of developing STS. Workplaces that are dictatorial prohibit candid discussion of difficulties and disregard the value of a healthy work-life balance may aid in the emergence of STS symptoms.

- Andrew D. discusses his excellent teaching experience at a Nevada school that addressed the health of instructors and kids outside the classroom. He stated: "Until my last two years of teaching, I worked in schools where most of the students had experienced trauma, and in North Las Vegas, they had these amazing support systems for the instructors who teach there." The urban teacher mentor program was one program I participated in. They established a support group where we would meet with new teachers after school, and they paired up more unique instructors with someone with numerous years of experience instructing in those types of schools. All of us could see that the district employs him, and he does not answer to the principal. Because they did not have to worry about it being evaluated, everyone could share their experiences of what was happening in the classroom. He came around to send teachers home at the end of the day and instructed them to talk at lunch, play, discuss what was going on in their lives, and have a real lunch break. He could provide us with plans and ideas to ensure we lived our whole lives outside school. That was very dissimilar to any other school I had ever taught. The principal would send emails on the weekends or at night, but that didn't happen at that school. At other schools, tutoring students during your lunch break or working through lunch was a badge of pride. They pushed you to take breaks, exercise, and practice mindfulness, and it made a significant difference." Which of these risk factors related to your work environment apply to you?

1. My employer encourages working after hours at home.

2. My employer has few resources for addressing recipients' mental health.

3. My employer encourages working through lunch.

4. My employer doesn't value having a work-life balance.

5. My employer doesn't encourage open communication about perceived problems.

6. None of these factors apply to my workplace.

Knowing the factors that can increase your risk for STS, such as working with traumatized patients, your personal experiences and character traits, and an office setting where wellness isn't prioritized, you may wonder if you currently have STS or if you suspect you do but are unsure of how severe it is. Be at ease. You can gauge your present syndrome level by measuring the three most common STS symptoms - thought intrusion, avoidance, and arousal at stop three.

ASSESSING YOURSELF FOR SECONDARY TRAUMATIC STRESS (STS)

Stop 3 – Looking at STS Symptoms

At stop number two, we discovered some STS risk factors and the explanations for why you might be susceptible to acquiring STS. Because of your employment, you can get to know your receivers quickly, and as a result, recipients occasionally confide in you about their personal life. This intimate connection can enhance your daily grind and benefit your work experience. However, poverty and trauma plague the lives of numerous recipients. Hearing these tales might make you feel quite heavy-hearted, especially if you believe nothing can be done to help the victim.

We might eventually start experiencing STS symptoms. For the rest of our time at stop three, we will discover how looking for STS symptoms in yourself is crucial. Then, we will learn how to look for STS in others. We will use a straightforward method to assess our SHAT (Support for Helpers Affected by Trauma) level, which involves answering specific questions about your current emotional state. We will calculate a SHAT score based on your responses. Your score's significance and suggestions for your next move will be explained. Finally, we will discuss how you and your organization might use this helpful tool to assist others. Why, then, should we check for STS in ourselves? Regularly monitoring our physical, emotional, and spiritual well-being can help us spot the early warning signs of STS, treat them before they worsen or develop into additional symptoms, and stop them from happening again.

The issues accompanying STS are another solid reason to heed its warning symptoms. There is a strong correlation between STS and burnout, according to studies. These studies showed that professionals typically experienced job burnout when subjected to secondary trauma. Job burnout occurs from workplace stressors that cause mental and emotional tiredness, which can reduce our productivity at work, as we covered in stop one. People who have STS may be more prone to developing substance use problems and depression. Lastly, STS can affect our everyday functioning and well-being. These typical symptoms can vary in intensity, but all are potentially problematic and can compromise our ability to do our job and maintain a healthy lifestyle outside of work.

We will soon learn more about how STS can impact us at work and home. You can determine your current SHAT (Support for Helpers Affected by Trauma) level by taking the SHAT level questionnaire and discovering where you officially fall on the STS scale. Based on your perception of your current level of work-related stress, where do you think you will fall on the SHAT (Support for Helpers Affected by Trauma) level scale:

- Little or None

- Mild

- Moderate

- High

- Very High

The SHAT level tool uses a version of a common standard STS questionnaire created by Brian Bride and his colleagues (Bride, 2007). We have adopted Dr. Bride's questionnaire for use by persons in the helping professions just like yourself. It comprises 17 items that ask about common symptoms of STS. Your individual "My SHAT level score" will correspond to one of five colors, each representing the severity of the STS you are experiencing. When we arrive at stop five, we will use this information to acquire further insight into options for self-care.

The green level means that you have little or no STS currently. For individuals at the **green** level, we recommend retaking my SHAT level once yearly or sooner if you have a secondary traumatic experience with a recipient or someone else.

The blue level shows that you have mild STS symptoms. We suggest retaking my SHAT level every nine months or sooner if you have a secondary traumatic experience with a recipient or someone else.

The yellow level shows moderate STS symptoms. We recommend monitoring your SHAT level at least three times this year. You may also benefit from consulting a resource list for what resources may be available, especially generating a self-care plan for yourself.

The orange level corresponds to a high level of STS. We recommend monitoring your SHAT level at least three times a year, for example, at the beginning or end of each quarter. You would almost certainly benefit from seeking counseling for additional support.

Lastly, a score at the red level indicates severe STS. We recommend monitoring how you are doing at least four times a year. Again, this could be at the beginning or end of each quarter or other regular intervals. Dr. Bride also strongly recommends seeking mental health care as soon as possible, regardless of your SHAT score if you scored in the **red** zone.

Regardless of which zone one falls into, the self-care strategies and the help to develop a personalized self-care plan we will create when we arrive at stop five can help keep you in the green or blue zone and help lower your score if you are already in the yellow, orange, or red zones. The questionnaire's results will include your overall SHAT level score and a breakdown of your present performance.

The three STS domains are **intrusion,** which is unwanted thoughts and sensations, **avoidance,** which is avoiding situations or objects connected to traumatic events; and **arousal,** which is a persistent sense of alertness. My SHAT level is finished in under ten minutes. Calculate your MY SHAT score right now.

Support for Helpers Affected by Trauma Questionnaire
(My SHAT Level Questionnaire)

The following is a list of statements made by persons whose work has impacted traumatized individuals. Read each account, then indicate how frequently the information was accurate for you in the past seven (7) days by circling the corresponding number next to the statement. NOTE: "Client" indicates persons with whom you have been engaged in a helping relationship. You may substitute another noun representing your work, such as consumer, patient, or recipient.

(1) Never   (2) Rarely   (3) Occasionally

(4) Often   (5) Very Often

- I felt emotionally numb…

1   2   3   4   5

- My heart started pounding when I thought about my work with clients …

    1   2   3   4   5

- It seemed as if I was reliving the trauma(s) experienced by my client(s)…

    1   2   3   4   5

- I had trouble sleeping …

    1   2   3   4   5

- I felt discouraged about the future…

    1   2   3   4   5

- Reminders of my work with clients upset me…

    1   2   3   4   5

- I had little interest in being around others…

    1   2   3   4   5

- I felt jumpy…

    1   2   3   4   5

- I was less active than usual…

  1   2   3   4   5

- I thought about my work with clients when I didn't intend to.

  1   2   3   4   5

- I had trouble concentrating…

  1   2   3   4   5

- I avoided people, places, or things that reminded me of my work with clients…

  1   2   3   4   5

- I had disturbing dreams about my work with clients…

  1   2   3   4   5

- I wanted to avoid working with some clients…

  1   2   3   4   5

- I was easily annoyed…

  1   2   3   4   5

- I expected something terrible to happen…

1   2   3   4   5

- I noticed gaps in my memory about client sessions…

1   2   3   4   5

Scoring Instructions: Several scoring schemes have been proposed, but a cumulative score of 38 or greater is positive for at least a moderate level of STS or vicarious trauma. Add up the numbers you circled to get your SHAT level score. Below is the "key" to see what color your personal SHAT level score level falls into.

Green = 17-27

Blue = 28-37

Yellow = 38-43

Orange = 44-48

Red = 49-85

Bride, B. (2007). The prevalence of secondary traumatic stress among social workers. Social Work, 52(1),

How did you score? If your SHAT level is green, that's great. Maybe you have not been exposed to the risk factors we discussed, or perhaps you are the person who manages stress more quickly than others. Self-care techniques can help you lower your score and possibly stop other symptoms if your score falls into one of the different colors on the scale.

Now that you know how my SHAT level functions and the insightful information it can offer regarding STS levels, let your coworkers see this workbook is available. My SHAT level can function well at an organizational level, just as it may be helpful in your self-care toolkit. When recipients are frequently exposed to stress or trauma or when a single unfavorable incidence significantly impacts the recipient's community, it can be beneficial for organizations. This can involve experiencing domestic abuse, a natural disaster, a crime, a fire, or another traumatic incident.

HOW STS MAY IMPACT YOU

Stop 4 – Six Main Spheres of Life

People who work in the caring professions frequently experience stress in their daily lives. Hearing about receivers' painful experiences and addressing their reactions to those traumas can cause STS symptoms. Even while these traumas haven't directly affected us, learning about, or seeing some aspects of the experiences of our recipients might make us feel as overwhelmed as if they had. It's critical to understand that this response is typical. Besides impairing your capacity to perform your job well, STS can also impact your emotional stability, close relationships, and physical health. Before exiting stop four, we hope you will comprehend how secondary traumatic stress can affect you across a variety of spheres of your life and be able to recognize its consequences. Let's examine how STS may impact the six main spheres of life: occupational, emotional, cognitive, social, physical, and spiritual. These domains naturally overlap and directly affect one another, but we will examine them independently for the duration of our time at stop four.

The most visible effect of STS is possibly in the **occupational** realm. Low morale and task avoidance habits at work may result from it. When performing your duties, you might avoid those who or things that bring back unpleasant memories for you. You can even start attempting to avoid your place of employment by calling in ill or working as little as possible there. You can discover that you are easily upset with coworkers and in the office. People with STS frequently struggle with feelings of loss, anxiety, melancholy, hopelessness, and emotional numbness over a more extended period. They also often had short-term sensations of rage and sadness. These feelings can occasionally be brought on by overt reminders of the distressing, traumatic events, but they can also sometimes appear suddenly and without warning. Over time, they can become such a normal part of our life that we might find it challenging to link the trauma exposures at work to their core cause. No matter how we feel about it, we probably won't be at our most productive if we have STS. How we respond to our symptoms may look like irritation and loss of patience with others and affect our coworkers by fostering negativity and dysfunction at work. We will now read a few examples of STS showing up within various professions and life domains:

- EMS technician John is sitting in his truck, feeling defeated. He is constantly reflecting on Liz, his most recent recipient. Liz, a young adolescent girl in foster care, claims to live in an abusive environment. After responding to a 911 call a few weeks ago, he recalls a situation where a parent may have burned his son. John remembers wanting to cry as the son described his sorrow and helplessness. Liz is another reminder of that talk, which he finds impossible to forget. John feels frustrated and helpless because of what occurred to Liz and how these memories still affect her. There are numerous reports on his work desk that he needs to type up, but all he can think about is how much he wishes he could assist Liz. When his walkie signals another run, he jumps, and when his teammate asks whether he is ready to roll, he snaps at him. Later that day, he becomes irate when a coworker forgets to hold a door open for him, and that evening, when he sits down to help his children with their schoolwork, he finds it difficult to concentrate and feels strangely disorganized.

It may be more challenging to control our **emotions** when we have STS. It might seem overwhelming to handle situations we would often handle without difficulty or react to with modest sadness, annoyance, or anxiety. We could become too sensitive to criticism and feel oppressed, or we might worry excessively even though we know we shouldn't. We might discover that trivial issues or conflicts make us disproportionately angry, which might cause disputes with family, friends, coworkers, or even the cashier at the grocery store. We can have dreams about the horrible incidents our recipients have told us about or notice that those events keep coming up in our waking thoughts. Events and behaviors from everyday life may trigger memories of past traumas, such as seeing a parent and child interact negatively while we are passing by, learning that a painful occurrence occurred, or hearing a tale that triggers memories of a traumatic event. These kinds of mental disturbances may lead to other issues. We could struggle to engage in activities we usually enjoy or to focus; we can become fixated on attempting to address the problems of our recipients. When we work to handle these unpleasant emotions, especially when we do not entirely understand why we feel them, we may abuse alcohol or other substances to self-medicate.

- Sylvia works in the medical field. One of Sylvia's recipients revealed two weeks ago that her father had gotten into a fight with her mother and had slammed her against the wall. The recipient was unclear about what to do and worried about her mother. Sylvia informed the authorities of her recipient's predicament. Sylvia typically takes excellent satisfaction in receiving input about her work. Still, something has frequently moved her to tears, and the suggestions made by coworkers and put on walk-through survey forms have irritated her. Sylvia's everyday responsibilities were feeling too much for her. She particularly dislikes being in crowded hospital areas, like the emergency room. She feverishly searches the area for unfamiliar faces when the noise level gets to her because she is worried that someone could come intending to damage themselves or other people. To handle her emotions of anxiousness,

Sylvia has become uncommonly impatient with her husband at home and has drunk several glasses of wine at night.

Our **cognitive** life domain, or how we think, is frequently impacted by STS. We often keep the details of tragic tales shared with us long after they were first told. Even when we do not intend to recall them, we do, most often in the worst possible circumstances. This could make it difficult for us to concentrate on essential things like finishing work assignments, supporting our dependents, or even simple tasks like grocery shopping or paying our expenses. Our capacity to reason clearly and logically and, as a result, to make wise decisions may be impaired. The cognitive effects of STS can be linked to these disruptions. Thought intrusion and sleep problems are two ways STS may affect and emerge in this area.

- Patty teaches 10th-grade social studies. As their final report in her class, Patty's students write about their cultural heritage and how their culture has shaped them. One of her students, Miguel, came to the US from El Salvador as an unaccompanied minor. In his report, Miguel shared his love of his native country and the struggles he experienced as he made his way to the United States. He discussed being smuggled into Mexico and having gang members extort money from him for safe passage across the border. He encountered days and nights of fear for his life and now suffers from frequent vivid nightmares. The week after reading Miguel's report, Patty mentally revisits his story several times daily. She worries about him and has trouble concentrating on even minor tasks like fixing dinner. At night she has nightmares about his traumatic journey to the US. Patty's principal notices she seems to have trouble following along during a staff meeting and has missed several deadlines for turning in lesson plans.

Socially, STS can interfere with the way we relate to other people. We may project negative feelings onto those close to us, mainly if we are unaware that we are experiencing STS symptoms. We may become distrustful and cynical. The behavior changes these thoughts and feelings cause, including mood swings, increased irritability, and intolerance, can push away the people in our support network when we need them most.

- Usually an enthusiastic, energetic young firefighter, Julio has taken to leaving right after work instead of debriefing the day with his team in the Workers Lounge. Instead of meeting up with his buddies twice a week to play basketball, he has been running by himself, turning down any offers from the company. Julio wants to help his sister through her divorce and feels terrible for failing her, but he cannot bring himself to answer the phone when she calls. On the rare occasions that he gets together with his buddies, he finds himself irritated by any discussion about potential work and relationship issues. He rescues people daily and works with people facing violence, losing their homes, and other hardships. He wants his buddies to see how small their issues are compared to his.

Socially, STS can affect how we interact with others. Ignoring that we suffer from STS symptoms, we may blame individuals near us for our bad sentiments. When we are at our most vulnerable, the individuals in our support network may become suspicious and cynical of us. The behavioral changes these thoughts and feelings bring such as mood swings, increased anger, and intolerance—can drive them away.

Due to our bodies enhanced autonomic responses and elevated stress hormones, STS can also indicate physical symptoms (Rauvola, Vega, & Lavigne, 2019). The body processes we are unaware of, including breathing, digestion, and heart rate, are all examples of autonomic activities STS impacts. We might feel our blood pressure rise, our pulse rate quicken, and our muscles stiffen. Chronic physical and emotional stress can cause headaches, nausea, weakened immunity, trouble falling or staying asleep, difficulty breathing, lethargy, or more sensitive startle responses.

- Shelly, a nurse in the emergency room, recently moved to a big city after seven years in her tiny community. Shelley had desired to work in a large hospital, so she was thrilled about the opportunity. However, she has grown highly concerned about the violence and the loss of some of her patients and their families after meeting a victim of domestic abuse at work. She has been taking over-the-counter medications for headaches and stomachaches since the second week at her new hospital. She also continues to reflect on these events. She has been having difficulties sleeping, replaying the stories she heard repeatedly, and worrying about her patients till the wee hours of the morning. She can hardly leave the bed when her alarm goes off, and her neck and back are always uncomfortable and tight. She knows she probably needs to see a doctor but lacks the willpower to schedule an appointment.

The **spiritual** sphere is another area that occasionally goes unnoticed when we consider how STS has affected society. This is possibly the most private area, partly because our unique definitions of spirituality are highly personal. If we believe in a higher power, we can blame that power for the experiences of our recipients and puzzle over how such things can occur. We could drift away from our worship group. We can doubt ingrained beliefs and perhaps our very existence itself. We may be prevented from partaking in the spiritual activities that we once found comforting by cynicism and confusion about our place in the world and our values.

- Mr. Thompson teaches numerous subjects and is preparing to retire from a Catholic school. Thankfully, there have been no gun-related catastrophes at the school. The growing frequency of school shootings that Mr. Thompson sees mentioned in the news depresses him. He questions why there has been such a large-scale increase in violence. He believes that the world now is distinct from the one he has spent most of his career in. The worst he has experienced

are occasional fights in the playground or minor misbe-
having. He agonizes over the reasons behind these terrible
tragedies and fears that one of his school's students will
soon enter the classroom armed. Despite his successful
profession and happy spouse, Mr. Thompson feels nothing
makes sense. His conviction that he has changed lives as
a teacher wavers. He even wonders if his long-held confidence in a loving God has been incorrect, leading him
to doubt his religious beliefs. What if there is no God at
all? Then there would be no reason to go to church. He is
preoccupied with the situation of the world and his position within it. Consumed, Mr. Thompson's thoughts are
preventing him from concentrating on his post-retirement
goals and enjoying time with his family. He considers
talking to his wife about his sentiments, but he is afraid
she won't understand, especially given his recent questions
about their shared religious beliefs.

Look at the following statements and choose if the individuals rep-
resented are experiencing **Everyday Stress, Burnout, or STS**:

1. Jeanette is feeling nervous before a scheduled class-
    room observation.

2. Brandon is worried about the blood test results of his
    son Johnny.

3. Christina is feeling exhausted by her current workload and calls in sick.

4. Jayden is feeling underappreciated. He avoids the staff lounge and takes lunch at his desk.

5. Carly is losing sleep; she is concerned one of her recipients isn't safe at home.

6. Michael has difficulty concentrating at work after hearing that one of his recipients was sexually abused.

There are numerous levels of disruption that STS causes in our professional, emotional, cognitive, social, physical, and spiritual realms. Everybody has a distinct individual interpretation of that scale. Dramatic interruptions in specific domains and minor disruptions in others may occur for some people. These disruptions can alter our worldview, how we perceive ourselves, our surroundings, and our interpersonal relationships. Especially if our STS symptoms are less evident or have steadily worsened over time, we could be unaware that such adjustments are occurring. It is challenging to diagnose STS because some people might not even be aware that they have or are experiencing symptoms, making it difficult to diagnose STS. Admitting that even reading or hearing about a tragic occurrence in the life of our recipient might cause us personal trauma may be uncomfortable; however, it is essential to do so. Now take time to reflect on the effects of your own job experiences on your occupational, emotional, cognitive, social, physical, or spiritual well-being. Don't worry about how positive or negative your answers may be because the exercise promotes self-awareness.

How has your work with trauma-exposed recipients affected the various domains of your life? Think about how your overall view of the world may have changed because of STS and hearing about your recipients' traumatic experiences. Have your work or social relationships been affected? Your ability to handle stress? What is the role of spirituality in your life? Consider each life domain and journal your responses below.

Occupational

Emotional

Cognitive

Social

Physical

Spiritual

Hopefully, you can see how STS may affect your life now that you have a more excellent knowledge of how it might affect several life domains. The self-care techniques we will go over at stop number five will provide you with ways to handle and, in some circumstances, prevent STS symptoms if you believe you may have them.

CREATING YOUR
INDIVIDUAL SELF-CARE PLAN

Stop 5 – The Self-Care Crossing

Most of us know the value of self-care and are familiar with the word. We may have even advised friends, family members, or co-workers to look after themselves better. Despite this, we regularly cannot follow through on our words. Self-care has numerous benefits, but even when we are aware of them, we do not always apply them.

At our last stop, the self-care crossing, we will discuss what self-care looks like in different facets of life. We will discuss some of the most popular justifications for not caring for ourselves and consider remedies. Before leaving stop five, you will create your self-care strategy by determining what gets in your way of engaging in self-care. This is done by proposing ways to go around them and establishing individualized, thorough self-care goals. By creating this customized strategy, we want to help you prioritize self-care and incorporate it into your personal and professional lives.

The word STS has been used since the 1980s (Rauvola, Vega, & Lavigne, 2019) and has always been a part of what it means to help and serve beneficiaries. STS can become commonplace as we establish trusting relationships with our recipients. I do this so they can share their stories of hardship and pain. Even for the most seasoned professionals, hearing these kinds of stories again can be detrimental and have long-lasting effects on the emotional and physical health of persons in the caring and serving professions. Unfortunately, numerous people believe that the best approach to handle being exposed to the suffering of others is to downplay or ignore any uncomfortable symptoms we may have. Because our beneficiaries suffer through these challenging times, we could feel we do not have a right to be anxious, upset, or furious. However, hearing about other people's suffering can also harm us, not that we cannot be strong or weak. Understanding how secondary traumatic stress affects each of us personally and taking steps to protect ourselves are essential components of resilience.

Self-care is a crucial element in the procedure. Self-care is a broad notion that can mean different things to different people, such as getting a good night's sleep, jogging, or getting regular massages. All these things could be essential components of a self-care plan. Self-care is more than just one practice or ingrained habit. In a perfect world, self-care encompasses all facets of our existence, including the ones that are professional, emotional, cognitive, social, physical, and spiritual.

Occupational:

Most people in your chosen occupation pursue careers to help and serve others. They have already given their all to the task at hand. They enjoy the difficulties of their jobs because they are interesting, but when a population is constantly in need, this can smother and finally kill that passion. Occupational self-care preserves and promotes professional engagement and enjoyment, even in complicated circumstances. We could feel more invested in our work if we sought professional development opportunities and made time to talk to our coworkers about issues at work. Similarly, seeking chances to consider successes and problems with coworkers from other businesses like ours might help us feel more professionally well-adjusted.

Occupational Self-Care Activity:

Which occupational self-care practices are you ready to engage in, do you currently practice, or think you could be prepared to engage in?

- Meet frequently with coworkers to support one another.

- Attend a professional development program.

- Read professional journals or books.

- Consult with someone more experienced.

- Unplug from work during vacation.

- Set boundaries for your time, such as leaving work at the planned time or taking time off.

Emotional:

The maintenance of emotional homeostasis requires developing resilience. Resiliency is the ability to bounce back rapidly from setbacks (Feldman, 2020), and emotional self-care refers to the coping mechanisms that either boost or reinforce our resilience levels. We can take care of our emotional well-being by finding a hobby we enjoy, volunteering in the community, practicing meditation, making art or writing, talking to a therapist, or spending time in nature.

Emotional Self-Care Activity:

Consider what you do to relax after a tough day on the emotional front. What settings or activities help you unwind after a tough day at work? Which dynamic self-care exercises can you do over the next few weeks?

- Discuss a difficult circumstance or a sufferer with a dependable coworker.

- For a change of scenery during lunch, go somewhere new.

- Set aside five minutes daily for stretching, deep breathing, or muscle relaxation.

- When you take a break, lock the door, and unwind (listen to music or read, for Example).

- If you are experiencing emotional difficulty, think about finding a therapist.

Determine what you will do in the upcoming weeks by reflecting on your chosen activities. Have you ever wished to read a particular book? A new place to eat that looks good. A park that you have seen but have never been to? Please put them in the spaces below.

If you said you had to be open to speaking with a colleague about a complicated circumstance or recipient, consider which colleagues you have felt most at ease speaking with. List those people below.

Who will you contact, either frequently or on a specific occasion? Consider the folks you would like to get to know better or who you would like to spend more time with. Type or write the names of those people below.

Cognitive:

A significant part of mental self-care is engaging in activities that mentally tax us and push us beyond our comfort zones. Mental self-care involves challenging our minds in new ways, such as learning new skills or registering for an online course on a topic we have always been passionate about. We increase our capacity to think creatively and solve difficulties by doing this. We may need to quiet our minds while we are experiencing STS. Choose a cognitive self-care activity from the list below that suits you. Which cognitive self-care techniques are you prepared to use, already use, or believe you might be ready to use?

- Read a nonfiction book about a topic you are interested in.

- Sleep enough to allow your brain to regenerate.

- Take a class on a subject that interests you.

- Stream a fresh podcast.

Social:

By practicing social self-care, we can develop wholesome, long-lasting relationships with others. When stressed, many of us distance ourselves from and avoid the people who care about the people we care about and us. A strong support network may encourage us to reach out when we have emotional trouble rather than withdraw. Intentionally celebrating significant life events with family and friends is one obvious way to build and maintain our relationships with others. Additionally, minor, and frequent activities are just as important. By taking time for regular get-togethers with friends or leaving work early to spend supper with our partner or children, we can deepen our social relationships with the people in our lives. If we have strong social relationships, those who know us well are more likely to notice when we are hurting and to contact us for support. Which of the enumerated social self-care activities below can you engage in?

- Gather with friends and family to commemorate significant occasions.

- Establish a regular day or time for your book club, coffee, date night, or stroll.

- Plan frequent outings (hikes, getting together at the dog park, going to the movies, visiting museums, and attending plays).

- Bring some friends to your favorite sporting event.

Consider specifics for the activity you chose when you respond to the questions below. You are likelier to stick to your strategy if it is more detailed. Consider the upcoming months.

What commitments can you make to the activities in your chosen categories (e.g., a monthly movie, an upcoming birthday celebration, a weekly walk, or the next neighborhood baseball game)?

Pick some dates on the calendar. What days can you commit to a regular activity or significant event over the upcoming three months? Enter the dates in the space provided.

Who will you contact, either frequently or on a specific occasion? Consider the folks you would like to get to know better or who you would like to spend more time with. In the space below, type or write the names of those people.

Physical:

People usually prioritize good self-care by starting with the physical components. This might be where developing a new healthcare habit is the easiest because most of us already know what good physical self-care looks like. Maintaining a regular sleep pattern, adopting healthy eating habits, and engaging in exercise, such as walking with a friend a few times weekly after work, are fundamental improvements. They may considerably impact our ability to cope with the challenges we face every day. Pick a routine action from the list below to help you get started on your commitment to schedule more physical self-care into your day. Start simple, pick an activity that fits into your daily schedule, and think about telling someone else about your plan so they can hold you accountable.

Which physical care actions listed below; can you commit to conducting?

- Take a walk.

- Pre- or post-work yoga classes are recommended.

- Take a stroll during lunch.

- Ride bicycles with your family as an activity.

- Jog with the dog.

- Stretch or engage in 10-minute workouts while watching TV.

Choose a day or hour to perform your chosen activity. You will be more likely to follow through on your plan if you arrange a specific time rather than just saying you will do it "sometime today." Type or write the date and time in the space below.

Consider who you might invite to join you if the activity is something you can do with a partner. The likelihood of performing a planned action rises when you are accountable to someone else, such as a friend, family member, or coworker. Type or write their name in the space below.

Spiritual:

Even while the phrase "spiritual self-care" can imply various things to different people, it refers to the process by which we learn for ourselves what it means to live or why we are here. This can involve developing or refining our faith in a higher power. A few ways to achieve this include self-reflection, meditation, prayer, attending church, reading about spiritual pursuits, and speaking with others about them. As part of your self-care strategy, concentrate on whatever is most helpful to you in your life.

Spiritual self-care may be a thoughtful, refreshing approach to caring for oneself regardless of your faith or religious convictions. Which spiritual self-care techniques do you intend to use, already use, or believe you might use?

- Spend ten silent minutes at the beginning of each day reflecting on a motivational book.

- Before entering a problematic scenario, be conscious of taking some time to meditate or pray.

- Attend a regular spiritual meeting or service to replenish oneself.

- Listen to music that is calming to the soul or is spiritual or meditative.

- Spend some time outside.

These fields don't differ from one another, and all of them overlap to varying degrees. Any self-care practice can benefit many things. For some people, going on a mountain excursion is an excellent form of physical exercise and a place of spiritual solace. While continuing education may require cognitive and occupational skills, meditation has spiritual and emotional benefits. Many know that taking better care of ourselves will benefit us in various aspects of life, yet we struggle to put this information into practice. Why do we not act when we know it will improve our well-being? Let's focus on the three fundamental barriers to developing self-care routines: time, guilt, and motivation.

Despite frequently claiming to want to do so, few people seem to have the time. However, time is not the issue. Self-care often feels like a luxury since there always seems to be something more important to accomplish, even though it is more correct to say that taking care of oneself comes first. Self-care must transform from something we might do when we have free time to something we must constantly do. Time must be weighed against worth. We carve out time each day for the important things to us. If we give self-care the same importance as eating, sleeping, and going to work, we will find the time to do it.

This leads us to the second time-related barrier to self-care: our propensity to see it as one-sided. If we cannot find the time to walk for an hour every day or to meditate for 20 minutes in the morning, we would prefer to do nothing at all. Instead, try breaking up your self-care into more manageable periods. Instead of walking for an hour, try incorporating walking into your usual routine. Park in the back of the lot when you shop or stroll for 10 minutes during lunch. Instead of feeling like you need to meditate for 20 minutes, take a break for 60 seconds three or four times throughout the day and take some deep breaths. No matter how little time you devote to self-care, it should have a significant positive impact, every bit matters.

Self-care is further complicated by guilt. We think that by prioritizing our wants over those of our friends, family members, and beneficiaries, we ignore them. Ironically, we embarrass ourselves so much that we refrain from doing things that would allow us to be more present for those individuals. If you have ever flown, you have probably heard a flight attendant tell you to put your oxygen mask on before helping others. Self-care is no different. When we prioritize our needs over those of others, we cannot help the people in our lives. Conversely, we have even more emotional energy to support others when caring for ourselves. Another way to eliminate guilt from the self-care equation is to make self-care a regular part of our daily routine, like brushing our teeth or getting the first cup of coffee.

Establishing and maintaining new behaviors takes time. When you lack motivation, give up on your self-care plan. You are more likely to succeed if you list the self-care practices you think you can maintain and have a simple strategy for incorporating them into your schedule. Consider also telling a family member, friend, or coworker about your plan and asking them to get back to you in about a week. Making a promise to someone else could motivate you to keep it. As you experience the effects of incorporating more specific, more doable self-care activities into your daily life, you could be encouraged to take on more challenging self-care goals. Let's read about the lives of the four people we met at stop number four: John, an EMS worker; Sylvia, a medical professional; Patty, a high school teacher; and Julio, a firefighter. While reading, consider how everyone prioritizes self-care.

- "When I'm out in the field, I work like a crazy guy," John said. I work extremely hard, but I take at least a two-week break in the summer. I always go on vacation in the summer. I needed to recharge, so I put my phone away on my day off and spend time alone. I adore massages. I enjoy reading. I love seeing movies and spending time with my loved ones. When I'm working or on call, I don't see them as often, but they are used to it. Drinking a lot of water during the day is beneficial. I exercise, try to sleep, or do something I'll probably enjoy when I can.

- Sylvia, a professional in the healthcare field, said: "Self-care can be challenging to practice, and I think that the first one is, you know, time. Time is difficult because there always seems to be something more important to do. It's vital to let go of the notion that self-care is always selfish or self-indulgent, especially if you are having a trying day or it is a stressful time of the year".

- High school teacher Patty stated, "I believe that there is always work to be done, and there is always more work to be done, and there are always more people working there. Since the district expects you to be available for the needs of students, I believe that for you to practice self-care, you must understand how crucial it is on your own. I believe you should know it. Working in a school where healthcare is valued is also necessary. We must practice self-care in school since many people who enter these helping professions struggle to say that they have too much to handle or do not have enough time to devote to their work. Working somewhere where that is respected is crucial if we are to care for our students".

- Long-time firefighter Julio said, "There are times when practicing self-care is tough. Since there are so few firefighters at the fire station, we are expected to perform all duties. We manage companies, and on top of our workloads and everything else, we are also supposed to give back to the community. I head the volleyball team and coach volleyball, so I have a lot going on. Because of this, it isn't easy to practice self-care because you want everything to go well. Therefore, it's challenging to exercise self-care. We concluded we needed to begin a procedure where we assign accountability partners among the firefighters. Together, we could listen to materials that encourage self-care, and occasionally, we check in with one another by asking, "Hey, did you go do that today? Or what time are you going to do that?" Doing this for each other can be extremely helpful.

It is accepted that working in a setting where self-care is promoted plays a significant role in managing STS symptoms. Lower rates of STS can be achieved through working in an environment where one's contributions are valued, one's opinions are respected, and policies that prioritize self-care are instituted. Organizations might consider initiatives like regular peer support meetings or a peer support buddy system regarding self-care.

You can now create your self-care plan based on the six categories we have discussed thus far in this workbook: occupational, emotional, cognitive, social, physical, and spiritual. For each domain, you will be asked to set SMART goals. A SMART goal is realistically achievable, time-bound, specified, measurable, and attainable. Let's say you want to mountain climb more frequently at Mt. Timpanogos. Although it is a self-care goal, this one isn't detailed enough to assist. The plan might be changed to "I'm going to practice mountain climbing on Saturdays at Mt. Timpanogos for the next month." You have committed to spending 2 hours at Mt. Timpanogos every Saturday for the coming month. This provides you with a transparent, quantified approach. This strategy is practical and calls for one weekly visit. We have produced a sample plan to review to help you develop your unique self-care strategy.

Now think about any barriers preventing you from implementing your self-care strategy. How about daycare? Do you have any other Saturday morning obligations that might prohibit you from following your plan? Do you drive a car? List the challenges that apply to your SMART goal and think about how you might solve them. Use the spaces below to write out and analyze your specific SMART goal.

My Self-Care Plan

- *Specific* - Is your goal specific? For Example - I know when, where, and for how long I'll be working on my goal.

- *Measurable* - Can you measure your progress toward reaching your goal? For Example - I am going to Mt. Timpanogos every Saturday this month for 2 hours.

- *Achievable* - Can you achieve your goal? Are the Barriers to reaching your goal surmountable? For Example – I don't have any potential conflicts.

- *Realistic* - Is your goal realistic? For Example - I can set aside time once a week.

- *Timely* – What is the time frame for your goal? For Example - I will make the time available to do this every Saturday over the next month.

S(pecific)M(easurable)A(chievable)R(ealistic)T(imely)

What is your Smart Goal?

How is your goal specific?

How is your goal measurable?

How is your goal achievable?

How is your goal realizable?

How is your goal timely?

Use the spaces below to evaluate your self-care aim and propose potential obstacles to overcome and alternative solutions to assist you.

S(pecific)M(easurable)A(chievable)R(ealistic)T(imely)

Barrier #1

Solution #1

Barrier #2

Solution #2

Barrier #3

Solution #3

Ernest Hemingway stated, "The world breaks everyone, and after that, many are strong at the broken spots" (Garrett, 2022). We can feel harmed when we hear about the terrible things our beneficiaries have been through. While navigating compassion fatigue or secondary traumatic stress, healthy self-care practices can fill in the blanks and give us the emotional grit and resilience to move on to healing from the inside out and achieve authenticity.

Congratulations, you have made it to the end of Part I and are well on your way to understanding what STS is, how it can affect you, and what you can do about it, and are closer to healing from the inside out and living authentically while navigating compassion fatigue or secondary traumatic stress than ever before. Part II will build upon what you learned in Part I by having you dig deeper into your self-awareness, dreams, passions, and future. Enjoy!

PART II

I'VE NAVIGATED ALL 5 STOPS. NOW WHAT?

THINGS WE CAN DO TODAY TO FIND OUR AUTHENTICITY WHILE NAVIGATING STS

6

INSPIRATION FOR HEALING FROM THE INSIDE OUT

"Dream as if you'll live forever.
Live as if you'll die today."

—James Dean, (Springer, 2021)

Your existence is a priceless gift. You can choose to do anything you want, whenever you want, and whatever you want on your path to living your most extraordinary life ever while being aware of your STS symptoms each day. You can tell yourself things like, "I feel like I'm stuck in the daily struggles of my recipients right now," or "I have a hard time achieving my life goals." I want to do whatever I want, but how do I get there? Even though you might feel caught in your current life position, navigating through STS entails deciding everything right now.

You can achieve amazing things if you can see what you truly desire and let your dreams bubble to the surface of your mind. When STS infiltrates the six life domains, you will know it, and with this awareness comes the power to live the life you have always wanted. This can be accomplished by allowing yourself to dream dreams you may have previously been reluctant to. Some might say it's easier said than done, but you will learn what to do as you traverse part II of this workbook.

The ten quotes in this chapter have the power to alter your life. They will assist you in building the extraordinary life you desire. Consider the conversation after reading each statement, then put the advice for that quote into practice.

Add your interpretation to the quotes that can be found on the pages of this chapter. Consider what each quotation means and how you can apply them. Be prepared. Your finest life - your dream life - is just awaiting your pursuit.

We All Dream. Be Open to Yours!

"All human beings are also dream beings.
Dreaming ties all mankind together."
—Jack Kerouac, (Encarnación-Pinedo, 2022)

In Kerouac's opinion, people often fantasize about their dreams. He also said that since everyone dreams, our shared desire to fulfill our ambitions binds us to one another (Encarnación-Pinedo, 2022). Kerouac also believed our dreams are a personal means for us to understand one another (Encarnación-Pinedo, 2022). Every person in a helping or serving career may experience STS. But because we are all thinking and visualizing the same things about what we may do in life, we can all be successful in living our finest lives. What comes to mind when you picture living the life you want?

Knowing that we can all imagine the existence we desire to live is reassuring. To live our best lives authentically, it is even more crucial that we take the measures required to realize our ambitions. To be open to your dreams, think about the following suggestions:

Identify what is most important to you. Perhaps you aspire to buy a small piece of land with a simple house, tour the world, or start your own business. Consider your most sincere desires. Write the things most important to you.

Make your life a living example of your most cherished dreams. The finest wish you can make for yourself is to live out your dreams every day and to inspire others to do the same. To put it simply, pursue your dreams. Motivate yourself to think about your dreams every day. No matter how busy you are, take a moment to consider the intricacies of your life's dreams. Even better, you can do it every day of the week simultaneously. Take a moment to write about how you plan to accomplish this.

Recognize that it's normal to aspire and desire; for instance, if you receive a fifteen-minute break at work in the morning, you could use that time to reflect on your dreams. Dreaming is never foolish or infantile. "All people aspire to how they want their lives to turn out," as Kerouac once said (Encarnación-Pinedo, 2022). The same is true for you. Tell someone about your most profound dreams. It's motivational to hear yourself discuss your aspirations since it makes your true objectives more evident. Try it. Who will you discuss your dreams with?

Together, we are all living this life and striving to live it to the fullest while dreaming of our inner magic. STS can no longer be used as a shield. You may be unconsciously concealing STS, but you are unaware of it. Our subconscious hides to defend us. It will be simpler for you to enable yourself to be franker and more open with yourself and others about what you crave the sooner you accept this concept.

Choose Your Dream

"You can plant a dream."
—Anne Campbell
(Dixon-Woods, Campbell, Willars, Aveling, et al., 2019).

This short, straightforward quote packs a powerful punch. One interpretation is that you may draw a picture of how you want your life to look, no matter where you are. According to the quote, dreams don't just happen to you at random. What your plan will be is up to you. Try these suggestions to plant your dream:

Decide where you wish to live both practically and metaphorically. Being in the right environment to make your dreams a reality is crucial to bringing your dreams to fruition. What environment must you live in to make your dreams a reality?

Consider whether the work you decide to pursue makes you happier than it does nervous, disappointed, furious, or any other STS emotions that enter our life domains. A crucial component of your life is what you do with your time each day. Make sure it's beautiful and engaging to you. Follow your passion. What pursuits ignite your passion? Do you schedule time each day to complete some of them? Setting your goals involves giving yourself the time and space to pursue the things that excite, delight, and intrigue you.

Give your dream nourishment. Plan your life to reflect your desires. The planting stage cannot be passed until then. For instance, you might aspire to be a professional singer but lack time to enroll in singing lessons or apply for one of the many reality television programs. What could you do to make it simpler for you to introduce others to your love of singing? How will you give your dreams nourishment?

Planting your dreams may be a scary, thrilling, and energizing experience. They may also need effort and preparation to make them come true. However, you are one step closer to realizing your aspirations and living your best life by becoming your authentic self while managing STS symptoms.

Nix, the Naysayers

*"He was a dreamer, a thinker, a speculative philosopher...
or, as his wife would have it, an idiot."*
—Douglas Adams (Leigh, 2021)

This remark makes a powerful message while adding humor to the concept of dreaming. Someone will always try to put a damper on whatever you can imagine, and STS can do the same if you let it. Consider these ideas for how to achieve your highest aspirations despite the doubters:

Create a personal philosophy. You create your philosophy of mind when you allow yourself to ponder what might be. What is your philosophy?

Recognize that not everyone will agree with your opinions. Use their criticism to motivate you to move forward and achieve your objectives.

Write the topics that often come to mind. Find recurring themes. For instance, you might disagree with the politics that many of your coworker's support. You can choose not to discuss your differences with them, but at least you demonstrate the most critical issues. Write the topics that are most important to you currently.

What do you consider to be life's most crucial elements? Have thoughts and opinions about issues, particularly those that concern you personally. Dream, reflect, and speculate. Refuse not to be discouraged by anyone. Continue speculating on your ideal existence, regardless of what others think or don't think. Instead of relying on people to motivate you to continue constructing your perfect life, give it to yourself. What do you need from yourself to live your ideal existence?

You will run into people who think you are insane, forever thinking you could attain your dreams on the path to achieving them. Accept that others might not see the connection between your dreams and reality but continue to dream. You might achieve your highest goals and live your finest life ever when you stick with it and stay committed to your dreams.

Leave Fear Behind and Go After Your Dreams

"All our dreams can come true if we dare to pursue them."
—Walt Disney (Miaw, 2019)

This little remark effectively captures what can occur when we pursue our aspirations. Walt Disney's narrative is exceptionally motivating for achieving your objective. Mr. Disney is undoubtedly a name that you are familiar with. He was a well-known business executive and cartoonist who, from 1927 until his passing, created, scripted, produced, and directed his television programs, as well as cartoons and movies.

Disney was a true dreamer, having risen from obscurity in Chicago to become one of the most well-known Americans in the world. Disney undoubtedly started dreaming at a young age and kept dreaming all his life. Disney's aspirations are shown in the countless cartoon characters he produced, with Mickey Mouse being one of his original creations. Other examples are Walt Disney World in Florida, Disneyland in California, Tokyo Disney, Euro Disney, Hong Kong Disneyland, Disney Paris, and Shanghai Disneyland were all established because of his desire to spread his art, joy, and storytelling.

Walt Disney's life, and the years following his passing in 1966, demonstrate the strength and potential of dreaming. Walt Disney's living children and grandkids have continued to perform his brother Roy's visions and hopes for the future even after Roy's passing. Walt Disney's ambitions have an enormous depth and breadth and extend into the future, and they are living examples of what may occur when your goals are pursued.

Disney considers courage as a crucial prerequisite for realizing ambitions in his remark. His assertion proves if you have the guts to pursue your goals, you can realize your aspirations. You can follow those goals by using the following techniques: Be courageous. Take a chance rather than be fearful. Be bold enough to start working on your objectives. Expect to experience worry and anxiety as you move forward, despite being cautious.

Establish a vision board. Create a vision board with images of everything you want in your life as your thoughts and ambitions become more concrete. Collect some poster board at your neighborhood dollar store. Glue magazine or newspaper clippings to the poster board that illustrate your viewpoint. Write and draw on it as you comment. Yes, you can create one online, but doing it the old-fashioned way will enable you to see your incredible life correctly.

Make a move. Whatever it is you want, go after it with all your might. Act every day to go closer to your desired outcome. Read about your interests, for instance. Discuss your dreams with people who are active in the same activities. Imagine what your life will be like once you have reached your goals.

Think of obstacles as challenges. Expect challenges to your objectives. Remember that overcoming the blocks will make obtaining your goal much sweeter, like navigating through STS.

Keep moving forward. You can move forward with newfound power and resolve when you think that all your dreams can come true if you have the guts and pursue them. Never undervalue your ability to fulfill your objectives. Consider Walt Disney, his life, and the beautiful things that have come about because of his fantasies. What can you do with your dreams if one man can achieve all of them with his?

Accept Your Part in Bringing Your Dreams to Life

*"If you take responsibility for yourself,
you will develop a hunger to accomplish your dreams."*
—Les Brown, (Blanchard & Broadwell, 2021)

This quote brings up a responsibility-related component of dreaming that you might not have thought of. By accepting responsibility for yourself, you agree to take charge of your life and make the decisions that will affect it and how you act with this responsibility given to you.

Brown uses the word "hunger" (Blanchard & Broadwell, 2021) to describe one's inner drive to realize one's aspirations, which is an intriguing feature of his quotation. When we are hungry, we seek food and continue seeking it until we locate it. Brown believed you would be motivated to achieve your goals when you fully own your life and decisions (Blanchard & Broadwell, 2021). Put the ideas expressed in this quote into practice by responding to the following inquiries:

Do you accept accountability for your actions? It would be best to refrain from holding people responsible for your decisions to achieve this. When you accept responsibility, you are more likely to take the necessary action to ensure that things turn out as you would like.

Maybe the objectives you have set for yourself aren't what you want to accomplish. If so, you can now spend some time understanding your true dreams. You can change your course to make sure you are moving in the life direction you want.

Are you following your dreams every day to satisfy your cravings? Pay attention to your feelings and goals. Allow your enthusiasm, desire, and "hunger" to dictate your behavior. Don't ignore the "hunger pangs." This will assist you not just as you make your way toward leading the most extraordinary life possible, but it will also help you as you learn to control your STS symptoms.

You are the owner of your life. "Life is what you make it." (Fox, 2019) This is a saying that everyone has heard. Here, your dreams are what you take responsibility for, think about, follow through with, and achieve. It is up to you if you can realize your dreams.

Share Your Dreams with Others

"It takes a lot of courage to show your dreams to someone else."
—Erma Bombeck, (Rizvi, 2022)

In this quote, responsibility is brought up, something you might not have thought about in dreams. Assuming personal accountability entails taking charge of your life and making decisions. Making judgments in your best interests becomes the "point person." Your decision to act is entirely up to you.

Bombeck's use of the word "hunger" (Rizvi, 2022) to describe one's inner motivation to realize their life goals is an intriguing feature of this quotation. When hungry, we seek food and keep going until we locate what we desire. According to Bombeck (Rizvi, 2022), you will be motivated to reach your life's objectives if you fully own your life and your decisions. Respond to the following inquiries, putting the ideas expressed in this quote into practice:

Just how "hungry" are you? Consider your life's objectives and the ideal version of yourself each day. Do you desire to accomplish these objectives in life? Are you compelled to pursue your goals fiercely? How come, if not?

It's possible that the objectives you have established for yourself are not what you want to accomplish. If so, take this opportunity to think about what your true dreams are. It is possible to change your course to move in the life direction you want.

It is your life, so own it. The saying "Life is what you make it" (Fox, 2019) has been used by all of us. Your obligation to consider, act upon and realize your dreams in this situation matters most. It is up to you if you can realize your dreams.

Ask Yourself, "Why Not?"

"Some look at things the way they are and ask why...
I dream of things that never were and ask why not."
—Robert Kennedy (Kennedy, 2020)

Whatever your political views, you have probably heard of Robert Francis Kennedy and thought he was interesting. RFK, as he was known, was a Kennedy family member who aspired to become a senator for New York before being assassinated in 1968. During one of his lectures in the 1960s, RFK said this. It is inspiring and helps one think positively.

This quotation provokes a lot of thought. RFK seemed to say that you should try to imagine what might happen in your life rather than merely watching from the sidelines and criticizing what everyone else is doing. It appears that RFK is urging us all to act in this quotation.

To present concepts that lead to your dreams: Imagine a problem and a solution. For instance, perhaps you believe that your current location prevents you from achieving your dream of becoming a singer. Where might you live, under ideal circumstances, to gain more exposure to musical theater? What is the next best place if you think Hollywood is the best place to pursue your singing dreams, but it is now impossible for you to do so? Perhaps you live in Tennessee and hold a position at a hospital, fire station, or school that would enable you to move to a bigger city, such as Nashville, where you might have more singing chances. Make some dream-related assignments. Using your ambition to sing professionally as an example, you may investigate Nashville to see the options for honing your talent. You might discover over 5–10 amateur and professional singing opportunities there. You may then travel to Nashville to check out those locations and speak with some of the staff members there. Plan out some modest steps you can take to achieve your dream. For instance, get in touch with the community theater where you live and start scheduling singing roles as soon as workable.

Based on his quote, some may claim that Robert Kennedy was the epitome of a dreamer. Consider how to live your best life and picture a means to live the existence you have long wished for.

Take Action Toward Your Dream

"A dream doesn't become reality through magic.
It takes sweat, determination, and hard work."
—Colin Powell, (Year, n.d.)

A well-known politician named Colin Powell made this statement about what it takes to realize your dreams. According to Powell, no magic can make our wishes come true. He felt that we must fully exert ourselves to achieve our goals and maintain our attention on the outcomes we want; we must fully exert ourselves. Your chances of realizing your dream increase with how hard you work and how long you persevere.

Implement these tactics to make your dream a reality: Do not think or desire that your dream will materialize magically. Instead, have faith in your strength. Establish a link between your aspirations and your efforts. Adopting a new mantra like "I hold the ability to create what I want in my life" could help you achieve this.

Work hard to build the life you want. For instance, if you are going to start your own business, put some effort into it by researching companies like the one you want.

Consult with others. Make a list of questions to pose to people who have established a life, business, or way of living as you desire; assemble as much data as you can.

Focus on the goal always. Staying motivated to attain your goals is simpler when you are clear about what you want and have developed an action plan.

Spend more time planning the life of your dreams. For instance, a few hours on the weekends can prevent you from entering your greatest desires.

You will probably need to invest a lot of sweat equity, time, and perseverance to make your aspirations and wishes come true. But if you are ready to put in the effort required to get there, you can live your most authentic life and release all symptoms of STS.

Create A Life That Truly Brings You Joy

"The most pitiful among men is he who turns his dreams into silver and gold."
~Khalil Gibran, (Gibran, 2022)

Gibran was an author, poet, and visual artist. He expressed his personal life philosophies through his many writings, including fiction, poetry, and short stories. Gibran emphasizes it would be unfortunate or even pitiful if one's dream were based solely on obtaining wealth in this passage. Gibran argues that pursuing your dreams should be done more for personal fulfillment than financial gain.

It will be fantastic if you make what you enjoy doing your life's work; however, it's wise to start choosing that career path based on your passion rather than the money you can make doing it. Take the following steps to seek a life you will love. Use your dreams as a guide to find your direction. Learn everything there is to know about them. You will see where you are going when you genuinely follow the rhythm of your proverbial drum.

Include activities that are inspired by your dreams in your daily activities. You will be prepared to engage in some daily activities related to your treasured thoughts once you access the content of your reviews. What are some actions you can do that are inspired by your dreams?

While pursuing your aspirations, keep your day job. Continue with your regular job until you are well-established in your dream profession to avoid confusing realizing your dreams with your ability to support yourself financially. Working on your plan and doing these activities will be an excellent resource for alleviating your STS symptoms.

Recognize that the time may come when you can live out your dream while earning money. However, refrain from using money as a justification for maintaining your desire.

Release your enthusiasm for what you want, then ride the wave of that passion to the culmination of your ambitions. Do not base your aspirations on how much money you will make. Instead, go for your treasured fantasies to sate your passion so you can feel the most unadulterated happiness you have ever known and live the most authentic life imaginable.

Make Your Dream Inevitable

"So many of our dreams at first seem impossible.
They seem improbable, and when we summon the will,
they soon become inevitable."
—Christopher Reeve (Chandrasekhar, 2021)

In his early 40s, Christopher Reeve was involved in a horseback riding accident that left him quadriplegic. Reeve continued to perform, write books and scripts, direct movies, and participate in activism for people with spinal cord injuries while being a person who has quadriplegia. As a result, Reeve's unique phrase sends a powerful message to everyone who dares to dream.

Reeve observed that when a dream initially enters your head, it would seem absurd even to consider that it could come true. Later, it seemed unlikely that it would ever happen. But in the end, if you decide to follow through on your desire, you realize the outcome is inevitable.

Continue with the following actions to position yourself for your desires to come true.

Provide a channel for your dreams. Discover strategies to communicate your goals. To represent them, take photos or paint something. Every morning, go for a walk and use the opportunity to consider how to carry out your idea. Spend ten minutes each morning reflecting on your dream. All these actions will be helpful to you as you navigate through STS.

Even if you think your dreams are impractical, keep going. Instead of pondering about them, move forward and overcome every difficulty.

Choose to go for your dream. Decide on doing modest things that are related to your life goals. You may even state, "I am bringing this about by taking all the necessary steps to achieve my intended goals."

Apply your suggestions. For instance, you can believe that helping those less fortunate than you are noble; however, you have not acted on this belief. It might be time to act on some of your suggestions. Create mini-goals and rejoice when you accomplish them. What could you do right away to move in the right direction if, for instance, one of your aspirations is a month-long vacation in Australia? Make a list of everything you had to do before the trip. You could read a history book about Australia right now. Then you can do targeted Australian tourist attractions research. Next, obtain information to guide your decision regarding your travel budget. Setting multiple smaller objectives helps motivate you to proceed.

A crucial step in achieving your life goals is letting your thoughts run free wherever and whenever they come to you. It would be best to first dream of reaching your goals; your finest life will have been lived before you know it.

Summary

"Do all you can to make your dreams come true."
—Joel Osteen, (Osteen, 2021)

These quotes are chock full of persuading ideas that may encourage you to keep working toward your desired glimmering life. They can aid you in navigating STS and its symptoms. Take what you will from these sayings. Apply the advice listed after that right away. Your ability to dream greater is increased when your mind is receptive to receiving novel or unexpected knowledge.

Your dreams provide inspirational ideas, beautiful experiences, and golden moments. Think of your ideal existence and try to get it! On the following few pages, you will discover a worksheet to help you get inspired to find your authenticity by healing from the inside out.

LIVING THE AUTHENTIC LIFE
OF YOUR DREAMS

You can start working for the life you have always desired right now. You can live the authentic life of your dreams and have the best life ever by completing the following exercises.

Accept the Fact that You Dream

1. What three life goals do you have which will help you fulfill your dreams?

2. How frequently do you consider your aspirations and objectives in life? Mark the answer that best fits your situation.

At least once per day

1-3 Times per week

1-3 Times Monthly

Every year – 2.4 times

Once a Year

Never

3. What are your thoughts about having and going after your dreams? Write it here. For instance, if you believe they are ridiculous, your goals are unreachable, or you do not have the time to achieve them, write what you need to fulfi ll your dreams.

Plant Your Dream

4. Do you live where pursuing your aspirations is simple? If not, list potential destinations where you could pursue your dreams.

5. How is your professional life? Are you engaged in a job that fascinates you or gives you fulfillment and happiness? What jobs or careers would you most like to have?

Regardless of what Others Think,

Pursue your Wildest Dreams.

6. Describe a few of your philosophies or the principles and ideas that are most significant to you.

7. Is somebody in your life who attempts to discourage you from pursuing your goals? Who, if so? How do you reply when someone refuses to accept, acknowledge, or even make fun of your plans?

8. What are three things you will do the next time someone doesn't take your dreams seriously? How can you respond in a way that shows how important your dreams are to you?

Be courageous and Follow Your Dreams.

9. For your aspirations, make a vision board. What tools will you require to complete it? List them here.

10. What steps will you take immediately to achieve your chosen life goals?

11. How will you react if you are hesitant or fearful about pursuing your aspirations? What will you do to show your courage in pursuing your goals?

Take Ownership of Your Goals

to Create a Hunger for Achieving Them.

12. How easily do you accept accountability for your actions and life?

13. What three things can you do to take more ownership of your actions?

14. What do you do when you have the impulse to work on your goals? Do you ignore the urge or act and continue working toward your goals?

Discuss Your Dreams Aloud

15. Have you ever discussed your aspirations for the future with someone? If so, what happened, and who was it? Who else can you share your dreams with?

Dream Big for Your Future

16. Here, you should describe your ideal future. Think about how your life will be when you pursue your goals.

Make a Commitment, Work Diligently, and Work Up a Sweat

17. What can you do to show that you are focused on your objectives and committed to achieving them?

18. List the three "work" things you can do to advance your goals.

Refrain from Making Your Life and Dreams

Entirely Dependent on Money

19. Write a few potential answers if your financial concerns prevent you from living authentically, such as how you might pursue your goals while leading a leaner lifestyle.

20. Conversely, is it possible that you may make some money while pursuing your goals? How? Until you're prepared to make significant life adjustments, consider keeping your current full-time employment and working toward goals "on the side" to earn a little money.

Call on Your Will to Realize Your Dreams

21. What are some of the ways you let your dreams come true?

22. Establish three smaller objectives to help you get closer authentically, heal from the inside out, and live the best life possible.

I PERMIT MYSELF TO ACT
IN MY OWN BEST INTERESTS

The affirmations below will help you find authenticity as you fight compassion fatigue and secondary traumatic stress (STS). Pick one or two of these affirmations and say them aloud each day.

- I am as important as anyone else in the world.

- I treat myself just as well as I treat everyone else.

- I purposefully give myself a high priority.

- I'm the only one who cares as much about my life as I do.

    o   I know I am responsible for leading my best life. I am responsible for the quality of my life.

- o Even though I care about others, I prioritize my needs just like others do. I go out of my way to help people, but I also ensure that what I do still enables me to care for myself.

- I choose my actions wisely every day.

- I don't give up too much when I help others. I'm just as important as they are.

- Before helping anyone else, I must take care of myself.

- People frequently put their wants first. If I sacrifice for everyone else, who will make one for me? I permit myself to act in my interests.

- Today, I place the highest focus on myself. I make decisions that help me live and achieve my desired future. I feel comfortable with the notion that I matter.

Self-Reflection Questions:

When do I give up too much for other people? Why do I act this way?

What do I hope to achieve in life? How much time and effort do I need to devote to improving myself to be successful?

What aspects of my life would alter if I put myself first?

I tend to My Requirements First.

- I make sure I satisfy my needs before I serve others. I understand my limitations. I know where I finish and where others start.

- I am conscious of my personal space. I respect my private sphere.

- I value and protect my emotional security. Before fully supporting others, I must tend to my needs. I honor myself. I celebrate other people. I first fill my cup; then I give what is left.

- I tell the truth while being kind to myself and others. I'm ready for feedback. I adhere to personal safety practices that I consider suitable for me while also thinking of others.

- Because of my compassion for myself, I also have an understanding of other people.

- I consider what is best for me before considering what is best for others. I'm skilled at balancing my desires with those of others.

- I have good thoughts about myself. I am sensitive to my feelings. As I learn more about others, I also learn more about myself.

- Since I am in honest connections with myself, I am in authentic relationships with others.

- I appreciate my beauty, making it easier to respect others' beauty. I realize peace inside myself manifests itself in my dealings with others.

- I now realize that by taking care of myself first, I will have the energy and resources to care for others.

Self-Reflection Questions:

Why is it crucially critical to put my oxygen mask on first?

2. How can I benefit from establishing clear boundaries with others?

3. Where can I test new limits when establishing clear boundaries with others? Home? Work? Friends?

9

NAVIGATING MY WAY TOWARD MY BEST LIFE EVER

10 Ways to Create an Incredible Life

Everyone once dreamed of living the life that would make excellent fiction. Unfortunately, many of us have exactly the life we want to avoid. Fortunately, it is never too late to start a fascinating adventure for yourself and change your life! Follow the advice given below to make the most of your time and lead a life you will never forget:

- **Take chances in challenges**—your creativity and intelligence increase when you focus your attention. Trials supply the potential to advance in your life. The more challenges you conquer, the better your life will be.

- **Be courteous.** Everyone you encounter has something to offer you. It can entail sharing important information, setting you up with the ideal person, or getting you the job of your dreams. You will lead a more fulfilling life if you show compassion and respect to everyone.

- **The Pareto Principle** should be followed. Everybody thinks each day is too brief. It's false, to put it simply. Said most people don't effectively prioritize their time. You can expect that most of the remaining 80% of your time will be wasted. Focus your attention on the 20% of the population that is most important (Kheybari, Naji, Razaie, & Salehpour, 2019).

- **Find a mentor.** Consider finding someone who is already leading the lifestyle you desire. Discover what they think. (It makes no sense to take advice from someone who hasn't achieved what you aspire to.)

- **Set objectives.** It would be best to focus your time, energy, and attention. Your goals provide that direction. If you do not have any goals, it won't matter if you are talented, competent, or endearing. Plan your path and select a few goals.

- **Be in the moment.** Both the past and the present are filled with regret and anxiety. Learn to be attentive by engaging in activities like yoga and meditation to keep your focus on the here and now and to steer clear of both.

- **Do not worry about what others may think.** Although it can be complicated to believe, most people don't always think about you. They are focused on their problems. You are more liberated than you might think!

- **Predispose yourself to action.** You probably know a few lovely, educated, and accomplished people who have trouble managing their lives. If you think more than you do, life will pass you by. After careful consideration, make a wise decision, and then work!

- **Smile.** You become friendlier and happier when you smile, and it's free. Try to grin everywhere you go for a week and observe the change.

- **Spend money on experiences instead of objects.** Today, far too much emphasis is placed on possessions like houses, cars, boats, and other status symbols. Even though these things are fun, your life will be more exciting and filled with beautiful experiences if you focus on your experiences instead of things.

Now is the right time to make some changes. Your life may have been very mundane and unremarkable until this moment. You may be struggling with STS. Choose what you are going to do moving forward. Create an authentic and fantastic life for yourself while having the experience of a lifetime. You'll find that managing STS and leading your best life has never been simpler by doing.

Ways to Look After Yourself While Being a Caregiver

If you've ever flown, you may be familiar with this safety warning: "Oxygen masks will drop in front of you if so and so happens." Please put on your masks before attempting to help anyone else. Do you recognize this instruction even if you've never been on an airplane? What are your thoughts?

You could believe it is simple to comprehend. But it's not for everyone. People who care about others are more likely to disobey this command, which is one reason. Why? They might wish to put their loved ones' security fi rst. Take parents as an illustration. They might choose to put their children's masks on fi rst most of the time. Even if this is a beautiful act of aff ection, consider the dangers. A father can pass out from oxygen deprivation before securely securing his child's mask. Both the parent and the child are in trouble if this occurs. Do we perceive a benefi t to following this instruction? We do. Would you believe me if I told you that even outside the confi nes of an airline, you could still benefi t from pursuing that fundamental rule? You certainly can. One area where it will be helpful is to apply this information to everyone in a helping and service vocation. Concentrate on this moment and consider how those who oversee caring for others can profi t by understanding this.

The Value of Looking After Yourself

Giving care to others can be fulfilling. A fundamental value and what most caregivers strive for is to be available to their recipients when they need you. Alternatively, giving care could be detrimental to your physical and mental health. Stress that leads to burnout is a condition that most caretakers eventually experience. As a caregiver's health deteriorates over time, their happiness may decline. How may a caregiver prevent this from taking place?

You've heard the adage, "Help yourself first, then others"? If we don't take care of ourselves first, how can we expect to help others effectively? Taking care of oneself is a crucial and much-ignored action that caregivers can take. Long-term harm will result if you ignore this. Think about the things listed below that service professionals can do to ensure they are taking care of themselves just as they are taking care of others:

- Develop compassion for yourself. Being gentle to oneself is the cornerstone of self-care.

- Praise yourself for completing the challenging work of serving and assisting others. Perhaps you are very critical of your efforts but work on getting past that part of yourself.

- Give yourself time to care for yourself, even for a few minutes each day. As you take care of yourself, you could feel guilty about it. If that occurs, remember that you can focus and be more effective when you do this. That ultimately helps both you and the people you are taking care of.

- No matter how much you enjoy helping others, remember that everyone has their limits. Don't allow yourself to become burnt out by disregarding your needs.

- Take a break when you need to decompress, especially if you discover you might be exhibiting STS symptoms.

Managing this can be challenging. You can feel emotionally spent because of your affection or empathy for the people you serve. So, seek out means of refueling. For instance, it's been proven that deep breathing makes us feel more relaxed. Why not make this part of your daily routine? You pay greater attention to your needs when you make time for yourself. You can carry them out once you are aware of them. Ultimately, you and the people you care about will be happier.

Make plans to stay healthy. When ill, caregivers are unable to complete their responsibilities. To perform at your best, your physical condition must be excellent. Another crucial component of self-care is this. How do you take care of yourself? To maintain your health, set goals for yourself. One of them might be a restful night's sleep. Keep yourself active by working out every day. The benefits will last a lifetime if you can do it even for ten minutes. Answer the following two questions and note that although they may sound alike, they are very different.

1. How do you care for yourself?

2. How will I care for myself?

Examples of things you can and perhaps should be doing are listed below.

- Schedule routine examinations. Getting professional counsel could help you identify your health's problem areas. Our happiness depends on our health. We can work more effectively when we take care of it.

- Enjoyable leisure activities should be pursued. A relaxing hobby can include reading an excellent book or having a warm bath. Remember that it is okay to prioritize your goals and wishes when you are a caregiver.

- Participate in activities that you find enjoyable outside of work. This can reduce any tension that you might feel while providing care.

- Continue to be socially connected. Maintaining connections is another aspect of self-care. You might join a support group if you can't enjoy the company of friends or family. There might be one in your neighborhood for caregivers.

- Maintain communication with your loved ones or pals. Share your thoughts and the difficulties you are facing. If you have any problems, the support they provide can be helpful. You might even avoid burning out if you do it.

You might care for a loved one or work as a service provider. As previously mentioned, remember that your tireless efforts could wear you out. Therefore, it only makes sense to take action to recharge your batteries. Both you and the people you care about need to be taken care of. You will remain healthy and content if you do this. It will guarantee that your loved ones receive the care they require. Additionally, it will provide you with the energy you need to continue working on your crucial tasks. Create an action plan based on these suggestions and write them below.

Give Yourself a Self-Concept Makeover

Your existing way of life is a direct result of your self-perception. You won't if you think you can't make a good livelihood. Your social life will be miserable if you think people dislike you. Your self-concept acts as a roadblock. You must remove the barrier first if you want to go beyond it.

Your past, present circumstances, and personal behaviors all shape your limitations. Thankfully, they are practical obstacles that can be surmounted with diligence and perseverance. After finishing, you'll be well on your way to leading the best life you've ever conducted. Buddha once remarked, "You deserve your limitless love and affection more than anyone in the universe" (Gilbert, 2021).

REEVALUATING MY PAST AND FINDING MY AUTHENTICITY WHILE NAVIGATING STS

Everyone carries the weight of unpleasant memories from their past. The most important thing is how past experiences are perceived and/or if some of these occurrences were our fault. Although it can be challenging, is the meaning we give to these events accurate? Additionally, is it beneficial? To become more authentic to ourselves, what can we learn from our past? There are several signs that you are not making good use of your past:

You keep doing the same things wrong. The past should be helpful. We can discover what works and what doesn't by accurately interpreting the past.

You don't consider the past. Although easy to carry out, the effects are not ideal. Not all scars disappear and get better. Are you currently being affected by anything from your past that you wish you could forget? Write your thoughts below.

Have you inherited any undesirable attitudes, convictions, or behavioral tendencies from your parents? Do you share your father's impatient personality, for example? Is your personality like your mother's, and do you routinely embellish the truth, for example? Do you distrust those who possess wealth?

Unchosen beliefs and attitudes might hurt how you view yourself. List those things from your upbringing and past that negatively impact you and write about what you will do to change that.

Is a single negative experience impacting your current set of beliefs? Even while these experiences are more likely to occur in your formative years, they can occur at any moment. For instance, perhaps you found your fourth-grade art class to be challenging. Maybe you've concluded that you're not artistic. Perhaps you believe your art teacher didn't like you or your art teacher was a poor teacher. Or maybe you think you're not a good person because you're not skilled at creating art. What negative experience from your past is impacting your thoughts and behavior today? What will you do to allow it to stay in the past?

You believe you have no imagination.

You find it challenging to learn new skills, so you believe you lack a lot of intelligence.

You believe people don't like you very much. Because of this, you tell yourself you will always be very cautious and circumspect, moving ahead to protect yourself from being criticized.

It is easy to comprehend how negative experiences could cause negative and erroneous beliefs. These concepts influence every element of your life and can severely limit you. Lucille Ball remarked,

"Love yourself first, and everything else falls into place" (Banks, 2022). You must first love yourself before you can accomplish anything in this life. Determine whether your past is seriously affecting how you view yourself. Please list below where you believe your past may seriously affect how you view yourself.

Make a list of your self-perceptions. Pay attention to any restrictions and constricting ideas. Consider all areas of your life where you feel restricted or dissatisfied. For example, I can't lose weight; I'll never have a healthy relationship; I'm bad with money; I lack self-control. If you go through these feelings, contest the assertion. This is an important step. Consider asking yourself where this idea came from. Is the source credible? Is there sufficient evidence to justify it? One encounter is frequently insufficient. One needs simply to touch a hot burner to arrive at a reliable conclusion. One failed romantic or commercial enterprise attempt is not. Is the belief reasonable, for example? Calculate the price of your faith. False beliefs can seriously hurt people. What do you believe your constraints to be costing you? Write your thoughts and impressions in the spaces provided below.

Pick a fresh angle to take. Choose a belief that fosters a positive self-image and more truly represents reality. "No one likes me" can be changed to "I can make friends easily." Take note to get evidence. In the previous example, even if you don't now have any pals, you can recall having them in the past. Consider a time in your past when you were more active in social situations. The idea that you can make many friends is a positive start. Defend your new conviction to yourself.

It's common to feel limited by the past. We frequently ignore that many of our self-perceptions are based on erroneous information. Walking and reading used to be challenging for you. Does that mean that you won't succeed today? The human brain solidly needs to interpret everything that happens. Sometimes that interpretation is incorrect. There is occasionally absolutely no meaning. You may heal from the inside out and find authenticity while navigating STS by reflecting on your past regarding STS and what we call "the bully in your head" (Williams, 2020). "If only you could understand how important you are to the lives of the people you meet and how important you can be to those you would never even imagine," said Fred Rogers (Harris, 2019). Every time you meet a new person, a little bit of you is left behind.

AUTHENTICITY, SELF-ESTEEM, SELF-CONCEPT, & STS – PUTTING IT ALL TOGETHER

Your self-concept and self-esteem are related even though they aren't the same. Your self-concept is what you think of yourself as. Your self-esteem may influence how happy you are with yourself. By raising the first, you can raise the other.

Boost your self-esteem and

increase your opinion of yourself:

1. **Set yourself up for success** by starting small. Success breeds confidence and a sense of worth in oneself. Create small wins in your life. Drink water rather than

soda during lunch. Pay all your bills on time this month. Starting small and feeling good about yourself is a great place to start. What small thing will you do today to begin feeling good about yourself?

2. **Try something that you may be nervous about.** Are you afraid of dogs? Visit a dog kennel. Are you reserved around other people? Tell a story to several friends immediately. Prove to yourself that you can push yourself over your existing comfort zone. List below things you are nervous about and what you are willing to do about it.

3. **Show off your skills.** Do you play sports well? Play softball in a league. Come on out and show off your abilities. It is a beautiful feeling when you accomplish something. Remember your strengths and capabilities. As a result, your sense of self-worth and confidence will rise. Additionally, a little boasting is entertaining. What are some of your positive skills and traits?

4. **Donate to others.** When you help someone else, you feel good about yourself. The average person worries a lot about being pompous or irresponsible. By assisting someone else, you can persuade yourself that you are decent. What can you do to help others, or what are you already doing to help others?

5. **Boost your diet's balance.** You become ill when you eat poorly. You are not feeling as good as you think. Simply said, you become used to it. Your mood and perspective on life will also improve as your diet does. What do you need to do to improve your diet?

6. **Avoid using analogies.** There is always someone more charismatic, wealthy, intellectual, or handsome. The world has a sizable population. Be proud of the life advancements you are making. What life advancements have you made? Writing them down will bring them alive for you.

7. **Learn some motivational facts**. It's easy to find publications, music, and programs encouraging optimistic thinking. If you routinely provide your brain with positive information, you will feel better about life and yourself. Keep away from negative news and people as well. What negative things should you avoid that could increase your happiness, authenticity, and positivity?

8. **Focus on your thoughts**. If you focus on your thoughts, you will be surprised and troubled by them. It's amazing how easily your mind switches between subjects and what strange things they can utter. Be aware of your unusual inner dialogue. What can you do to ignore the "bully in your brain" (Williams, 2020)?

9. **Make a list of uplifting remarks.** Make a list of affirmations you want to hold valid and always carry them. When your mind is empty, repeat your promises to yourself. When you are not doing anything, your thoughts will run rampant. Keep the discourse positive and under control.

10. **Recall your majesty.** You have come a long way! Make a list of all you have accomplished so far in your life. It is simple to lose track of your advancement. Review this list often.

11. **Find something new**. When they learn something new, children are very proud of themselves. Adults, too, feel happy when they learn to do new things. Never stop the process of learning. Start with things you know you enjoy. Periodically, take the time to learn something new even if you are unsure you will like it. What are some new things you would like to learn?

12. **Exercise**. You know that consistency is required. When you do not accomplish things, you become frustrated with yourself and doubt your self-discipline. Exercise can be fun. What types of exercise do you enjoy?

13. **When you meet someone new,** introduce yourself to them. This will give you a sense of control over your life, help you get over any shyness, and you might even make some new friends. Everyone has some level of apprehension around strangers. Lowering your anxiety will help you feel more confident and content with yourself. What can you do today to be more outgoing around others?

Everyone could use more self-confidence. You are better positioned to alter your life and self-concept when you have higher expectations of yourself. We could all use a little more self-assurance. When you hold greater standards for yourself, you can hange your life and your perception of yourself. Consider more strategies to raise your self-esteem and use these ideas consistently.

Andrew Matthews states, "A healthy self-love means we do not need to explain to ourselves or others why we go on vacation, why we stay up late, why we buy new shoes, or why we occasionally treat ourselves" (Matthews, 1997). We should be at ease engaging in activities that enhance the beauty and quality of life.

Improve Your Life

Making positive changes is one of the finest ways to enhance your self-concept and live your best life. It is easier to think positively about yourself when you lead a prosperous and full life. Having a 45-inch waist, eating instant soup every night, and living in a studio apartment are not always negative traits. However, happy thoughts are easier to find when you are satisfied with your life! Consider the most important aspects of your life, then attempt to improve. What are some improvements you would like to make in your life?

Wellness and Health

Are you as healthy and fit as you'd like to be? Being healthy offers advantages, even though having a 6-pack is unnecessary to show off at the beach. Anyone who values themselves should put a lot of effort into being healthy. A stunning physique also boosts self-esteem and demonstrates restraint.

- **Show yourself** that you are worth the time and energy needed to maintain good health.

- **Complete your** yearly physical with your physician or nurse practitioner Everybody should see their doctor at least once a year. Numerous medically severe conditions rarely have symptoms.

- **Self-care** demonstrates how much you value and respect yourself. Contrarily, an "I don't care" attitude demonstrates you do not value yourself.

- **Routine exercise** shows you once more that you are worth the effort.

- **Identify** a healthy weight and maintain it. Being overweight is unpleasant and can seriously undermine one's self-esteem. However, changing your body weight for the better over time is challenging.

- **Make small,** doable dietary changes. One such adjustment is to replace soda with water once a day.

Simply said, develop healthy behaviors one step at a time, do not rush it. Uphold a healthy way of living. Eat a balanced diet, exercise frequently, and see your doctor periodically. Self-care is crucial and enhances your self-concept and self-esteem. Stacey Charter counseled, "Do not place your happiness and sense of value in other people. You are the only one responsible for that. If you are unable to love and respect yourself, no one else can do it for you" (Russ-Eft, Bober, De La Teja, Foxon, & Koszaika, 2008). Make the changes you feel are essential for YOU, not because you think someone else wants you to after you have accepted yourself entirely, flaws and all.

Social Life

No one, neither a man nor a woman, is an island (Burger, 1970). Humans are social creatures; thus, you must include other people in your perfect existence unless it includes adopting a vow of silence and spending all day on top of a mountain. The quality of your social life influences how you feel about yourself. If you wish more people were eager to spend time with you, what can you, or what are you willing to do about it?

Soon, one's social life might be more fulfilling if you:

- Decide on the social life you want to lead. Being the center of attention and spending every evening with a large group is not for everyone. You could engage in a regular weekend social activity and maintain regular dinner dates with a few close friends. You are free to decide. Give it some thought and write it down.

- Discover what has been impeding you. As soon as you are aware of the cause, planning is feasible. I work from home, I don't usually engage with people, being timid, and struggling to communicate with others are a few examples.

- Create a strategy, then execute it. Books exist that discuss charismatic behavior. Videos on how to get over shyness or social anxiety are available. Maybe you should reach out to the people you already know. Perhaps you'll develop a brand-new hobby or join a social club.

- Create new connections in your social network one at a time. Many people only need a few close friends to feel confident and comfortable in this area of their lives. Write down what you can do personally to create new or strengthen old connections.

Building a satisfying social life is much easier than you would think. Never forget that loneliness affects most people to varying degrees. Howard Thurman Washington suggested we "Ask yourself what brings you life instead of what the world requires. Meeting people who want to leave the house and engage in a worthwhile activity or conversation is not difficult. The world needs people who have come alive" (Thurman, 1981).

Finances

It's challenging to feel good about yourself when you must figure out how to fill your gas tank for over $3 a gallon, for example. Your self-concept depends on you having the resources to pay for the necessities of life. Feeling horrible about yourself is easy when you can't pay your debts. Take charge of your money.

- Create a simple budget and stick to it. Everyone needs a budget regardless of their annual income, $10,000 or $10 million. Numerous publications and websites tackle personal money and budgeting concerns. Find out the information you require for yourself.

- Learn how to save. A realistic budget will leave you with extra cash at the end of the month. Save it and use it to make intelligent investments.

- Get paid more. If your income is insufficient to cover your expenses, your only choices are to cut spending or boost revenue. Your alternatives for increasing your income include earning a raise at your current job, switching to a better-paying one, and developing a primary or secondary job for yourself. Online opportunities are plentiful in the contemporary world.

- Take steps to establish the kind of financial lifestyle that appeals to you. Money is significant, even though it is not everything. You will feel more capable and less down if your financial position is stable.

Louise L. Hay observed, "You have been condemning yourself for years, but it hasn't helped" (Hay & Kessler, 2015). Try approving of yourself and see what happens.

Have Goals

Do you have any objectives? Possessing optimism for the future and steady progress in life will enhance your sense of self. Numerous studies have shown that those with goals outperform those without in every aspect of life. Having a few goals results in a sense of purpose, direction, and control. Setting goals is simple and effective:

- Set goals with a maximum 12-week time frame. More than this makes it challenging to maintain attention and motivation. If your goal is too big to achieve in a year, set short-term objectives to help you go in the right direction.

- Journal your experiences and progress as you go along this path. As a result, your goals will remain top-of-mind, and you will receive the feedback you require to work as efficiently as possible.

- Take inspiration from progress. To strengthen your self-concept, always try to feel good about yourself. Since most people have lived in the same neighborhood or city their entire lives, every success in life is a source of happiness. Write your thoughts about goals.

Setting goals might be challenging, but it does not have to be. Your self-concept can be improved by making steady progress toward a few objectives. It indicates that you have the power to affect and transform your life.

Give of Yourself Regularly

I'm not referring to the assistance and services you currently offer clients in your line of business. Your self-concept encompasses who you are and how you see yourself about other people and the outside world. A great way to enhance your self-concept and self-esteem is to give to others, expecting nothing in return. You could believe you have little time for anything else because you spend much of your professional life serving others. However, you can improve your self-worth and move closer to living your best life, overcoming STS, and healing from the inside out by frequently giving of yourself. Here are some illustrations of this:

- Offer to assist. Organizations are always in need of more volunteers. Choose a cause that appeals to you, then contribute.

- Find a position or side business that helps others. You could teach reading to adults or young students. Maybe you work with senior citizens one evening per week. There are several occupations accessible that significantly benefit others.

- Look out for how you can provide unanticipated displays of charity. In life, there are several chances to help others out. One cannot help but love oneself when performing a beautiful act for another.

- Continue being a good person. Think about an average day.

What little changes could you make to better assist or care for people? What would you like to do, if anything, to help others, and what is keeping you from doing it?

"The most attractive people we have ever encountered are those who have overcome failure, suffering, loss, and adversity. Because of their appreciation, sensitivity, and understanding of life, these people are brimming with compassion, empathy, and deep, loving concern. Beautiful individuals don't appear" (Kübler-Ross, 2014). What thoughts come to your mind when reading this quote by Elizabeth Kübler-Ross?

Who Do You Wish to Be?

Most of us have never desired to be an average person who works in a cubicle at a job we detest. When you become the authentic individual you have always wanted to be, your self-concept will be at its best for you. Doesn't everyone want something like this? When you become the individual you are striving to become, you will experience internal healing and lead a simple life. You will transcend the idea of a "self-concept." Consciously select your identity:

- Name a person you admire and explain why. Do you wish you were more like James Bond? Why? Are you a fan of Lincoln? Albert Einstein Why? Write and describe your thoughts below:

- What personal qualities have you always found admirable in others?

Charismatic or Self-Assured?
How resilient are they?
Kindness?
Adaptability under pressure or joy?

- How can you live the life you have always desired right away? You are unstoppable; no one can stop you. Anyone who tries to get in your way can be disregarded. Increase. Make it a point to behave as you would like to be emulated.

This is the goal. If you are the person you want to be and live the life you wish to, your perception of yourself will be at its finest. Everything else is only a stepping-stone to get here. "One doesn't convince others because one believes in oneself," said Lao-Tzu (Chan, 2015). When someone is content with himself, they do not need the approval of others. When a person embraces, the world follows suit.

Conclusion

How you see yourself now results from your past or your perspective of the past. Think back on your unpleasant experiences, then propose a more upbeat solution. Remember that the past is in the past and cannot foretell the future. The past is only a barrier if you let it be. If you raise your self-esteem, you will have the will to alter your self-perception. This process has already started. You already have a lot of good reasons to like who you are. Don't forget to tell yourself all the time how amazing you are. Improve your life in any manner you can. As you create and lead the life you desire, your self-concept will change, and you will begin acting the way you know you ought to. This is the key to having the finest sense of oneself. The highest point is reached when you can show that your behavior and ideas are consistent with your goal of the ideal life and person.

YOUR SELF-CARE CHECKLIST

You and everyone you know probably have a specific favorite color, flavor, place to visit, etc. It only makes sense that everyone would have a distinct ideal self-care checklist. Maybe a friend likes adult coloring books, but they bore you. Someone you know might want to reserve a spa package at a luxurious hotel, but you would much rather pitch a tent. For self-care to be effective, it must match your personality and lifestyle. Think about implementing these suggestions to design routines that are true to you. You get to pick who will look after you, and you get to choose who you are. Success tips include the following:

- **Become more aware.** How much do you know about yourself? Keep an eye on your feelings and thoughts and investigate them. Please consult with your friends and family for their opinions.

- **Management of time.** Be realistic about what you can fit into your schedule. You might be able to find more time for yourself if you wake up earlier and put your phone away for a while each day. Make a plan for yourself to manage your time in a more productive and life-fulfilling way.

- **Stick to your budget.** Self-care doesn't have to be expensive. Utilize free activities like walking or going to a park; however, you could find certain purchases valuable. What changes would you like to make to your current budget?

- **Keep a journal of your feelings.** Focus on your principles and top goals instead of trying to keep up with the latest trends. It's acceptable to use charcoal toothpaste and avoid green juice fasts. Why do you believe journaling is or is not essential?

- **Observe what fascinates you.** Incorporate your favorite pastimes into your everyday schedule. This may lead to more dancing parties or quiet reading sessions. What activities would you like to incorporate into your daily schedule?

- **Try something new.** On the other hand, be open to enlarging your areas of interest. Talk to your friends about what they are doing and try out some of the ideas you see on Instagram, for example. You might be surprised to hear that you like CrossFit or bubble baths. What is something new that you would like to try? What has kept you from trying this? How will you develop a plan of action now?

- **Achieve balance.** Think about the areas you might be skipping. You might work out frequently and yet skip stretching. You indulge yourself at home, allowing stress to accumulate at work. What are things you can do to bring balance into your life better?

- **Have a wonderful time.** It's great to use your strengths when you have free time but remember that there are no grades. If it amuses you, you only need to know that you were trying to fold an origami frog.

- **Refresh when required.** Be prepared for your self-care requirements to fluctuate over time and even daily. Change your plans whenever necessary. What are your self-care needs, or in other words, what self-care items would you like to be a non-negotiable in your life? How will you accomplish this?

While we each meet specific needs differently, we all share some things in common. Ensure that your self-care strategy promotes your general well-being.

Consider these strategies:

1. **Take good care of your body.** Maintain a healthy body. Stay within a healthy weight range. Eat at least five servings of fruits and vegetables daily as a healthy diet. Set a weekly goal of 150 minutes of moderate activity.

2. **Consider your mental health.** Be kind and compassionate to yourself, especially during challenging times. Ask for help when you need it.

3. **Do not be timid.** Establish a strong network of allies. Stay in touch with your friends and family. Establish proper boundaries and talk about your feelings.

4. **Spiritual growth.** Think about what you desire from life. Spend lavishly and connect with something bigger than yourself. Join a congregation or follow your principles.

You're more likely to consistently practice self-care if your self-care checklist is tailored to your unique mind, body, and spirit. When you put yourself first, your happiness and prosperity will rise as you give more to others.

Accept Who You Are – You Are Great!

The best course of action requires that you accept who you are. Accepting who you are is the first step in developing self-esteem, which leads to better self-care. Feeling comfortable about yourself is impossible if you cannot accept who you are. Your level of self-acceptance is determined by how pleased you feel about yourself. Many mental health professionals believe that before transformation can occur, self-acceptance is necessary. If you feel confined, lacking self-acceptance might be the first challenge to overcome. If you accept your flaws, you can change them.

Learn to accept yourself and enjoy the person you are:

Many individuals blame who they are or their frailties on their parents and upbringing. Don't do this. Put your past in the past if you can—the caliber of parents, siblings, or friends we had while growing up can vary substantially. For example, overly critical parents don't raise awful kids; that's how they were. Nothing will be accomplished by criticizing the flaws of anyone who helped raise you. You should forgive them and let go of the past to overcome this. Don't evaluate yourself based on your upbringing. Your upbringing may be reflected in you; however, your upbringing is not you. Here are some suggestions on how you can enjoy yourself:

- **Volunteer.** The simplest and most powerful way to convince yourself that you deserve acceptance is to offer your time to someone in need. To yourself, brag about your good character. Many volunteering opportunities exist in your community. Where would you like to volunteer?

- **Take pride in your abilities.** It's challenging to accept oneself if you constantly remind yourself of your imperfections. Make a thorough list that you can look back on. Write out all you can about yourself that is excellent. Any positive trait, no matter how tiny, deserves attention. Tell yourself…

> … "'I am a decent person."
> … "I am an empathetic person."
> … "I stand up for my friends."

What are your positive traits?

- **Be kind to yourself.** It is challenging to accept yourself if you are often emphasizing your imperfections. Make a comprehensive list that you can look back on. Make a list of all your strengths. It's critical to draw attention to even the slightest positive aspect.

- **Don't hold on to unattainable objectives.** If you are 57, your dream of becoming an astronaut is finished. It is. It may not be easy to accept who you are if your current life differs significantly from what you had in mind. When should you stop trying so much? Allow this moment to be that one. Make new, intriguing plans that you firmly believe in.

- **Stop talking negatively about yourself.** You can not accept yourself if you continuously make fun of yourself.

Give yourself the best chance to come to terms with who you are. Be honest with yourself like you would a reliable friend. Make friends with yourself. Write down your thoughts on how you can be a better friend to yourself.

- **Be genuine.** When you put on a character for the world, you do not give people a chance to accept you for who you are. How are you going to develop self-love? When you are being sincere, the affection you receive feels much more substantial. Being genuine is terrifying but easy. People who have the guts to be authentic are respected and esteemed. Write down your thoughts on being genuine.

- **Realize how valuable you are to the world.** Fortunately, you do not have to earn this. You are born with it. How much more could you provide if you made the effort? The universe needs you. More than anything else, what the world requires of you, speaks volumes about your inherent value. How do you bring value to the world?

- **Pardon others**. The ability to forgive others and forgive oneself are mutually exclusive. You find accepting yourself will be much easier if you practice forgiving others.

"Self-acceptance" is the term used to describe tolerating oneself. Nobody is perfect. Even if each member of your family and friends has a unique flaw, you still accept them. Give yourself the same wiggle room. Focus on your areas of strength while accepting your weaknesses. When you live authentically, others will accept you more for who you are.

The following chapters will lead you through several strategies to help you overcome the main roadblocks you will likely encounter on this part of your journey toward authenticity. The thought of accepting oneself could be complex. You will learn to forgive yourself, put your past wrongs behind you, exclude persistent self-doubts, and develop a good self-image.

Be proud of your strengths! In your journal, write every positive thing you can conceive about yourself. Reflect on how wonderful you are! Below are some of your most positive strengths, qualities, and achievements.

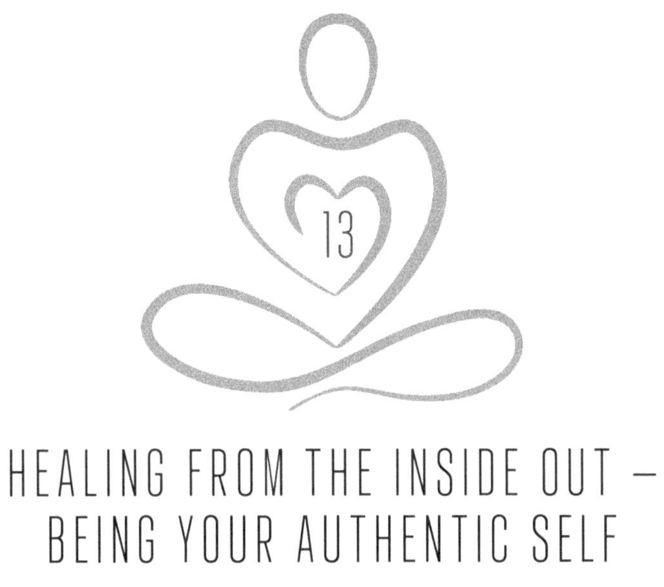

HEALING FROM THE INSIDE OUT – BEING YOUR AUTHENTIC SELF

Know Yourself – The First Step to Being Authentic

You cannot live authentically if you do not know who you are. Your self-awareness is crucial! What is self-awareness? According to the definition, self-awareness is "knowledge and understanding of your personality or character" (Morin, 2011). When you know yourself, you can recognize your personality traits, virtues, flaws, and beliefs accurately and clearly. YourDon'ttriggers are known to you. You must be aware of these triggers to avoid returning to prior non-authentic behavior.

Without self-awareness, life may be incredibly confusing and up-setting! Your level of self-awareness can impact your relationships, profession, and happiness:

- You must know yourself if you want to control your life. Your beliefs, emotions, responses, and thoughts determine your life'life'sction. Self-awareness is the key to understanding and influencing these events. Self-awareness gives you the power to change by exposing erroneous beliefs and irrational emotional reactions. What false beliefs and/or irrational emotional reactions keep you from being authentic and interfere with healing from the inside out?

- The underlying reasons for earlier failures and challenges are revealed by self-awareness. We frequently blame our failures on unfavorable circumstances or bad timing. It is also possible that we mistook the situation, other individuals, or even ourselves for something else. Honest self-evaluation makes it much easier to comprehend why relationships, careers, and other challenges are challenging.

- Do you frequently experience difficulties at work in your relationships? What can you improve upon?

- Those who are not self-aware are perplexed by their unfavorable outcomes or solely place the blame on others.

- Self-awareness reveals the fundamental causes of previous setbacks and difficulties. We usually attribute our shortcomings to unfavorable situations or poor timing. We can mistake the circumstance, others, or ourselves for something else. Understanding why relationships, careers, and other difficulties are complex becomes easier after being honest with oneself.

- Be aware of your deficiencies and what you are skilled at. Are you good at assembling teams, friendships, and associates who can fill those gaps; you will have more success as you become more self-aware. Make a list of them and consider how you can become self-aware.

- Your ability to lead is limited if you lack self-awareness.

- Self-awareness is the cornerstone of individual growth. Without it, any attempts at personal development will be significantly hampered.

- Self-awareness is the foundation for success and self-improvement. Your level of self-awareness will determine how well you use your information. You must be conscious of your beliefs, routines, abilities, and weaknesses if you want to undergo a personal transformation. Don't presume you are aware of yourself. What does self-awareness mean to you? How will you use self-awareness on your journey, navigating STS, being authentic, and living your best life ever?

Becoming more self-aware is possible, but it won't happen overnight. You can increase your self-awareness immediately and start taking charge of it. Make a list of your everyday activities and give each one a positive or negative grade. Then decide to change only one habit. You can determine if you wish to change a bad behavior or strengthen a good habit. Plan for how you'll stop the habit you've picked.

Top 10 Ways to Develop Self-Awareness

Self-awareness is also the ability to comprehend who you are entirely. It entails being aware of your habits, emotional tendencies, wants, desires, strengths, and weaknesses. Possessing a high degree of self-awareness is a powerful weapon. Since you are aware of your habits, you may be able to change your life more successfully. Those who are self-aware may find life to be frustrating.

Develop your self-awareness:

Notice your thoughts. Unless you have been practicing meditation for a long time, your mind constantly generates thoughts and remarks. You can't just say, "That's a magnificent tree," while standing in front of one. Take note of your thought processes. When you're anxious, what are you thinking? Are you bored, interested, or confused? You'll see that identical circumstances lead to comparable cognitive processes.

Do you consider people and situations? Do you often find yourself thinking about the past or the future?

Do you believe the worst, or the finest will happen?

Be aware of your emotions. What emotions are you experiencing today? What emotions do you experience as you eat? Taking a car to work? Lie down in bed? Standing in line?

Once you've become aware sof your feelings, probe them. Ask yourself, "how do I feel"? "Why"? "What do I currently require"?

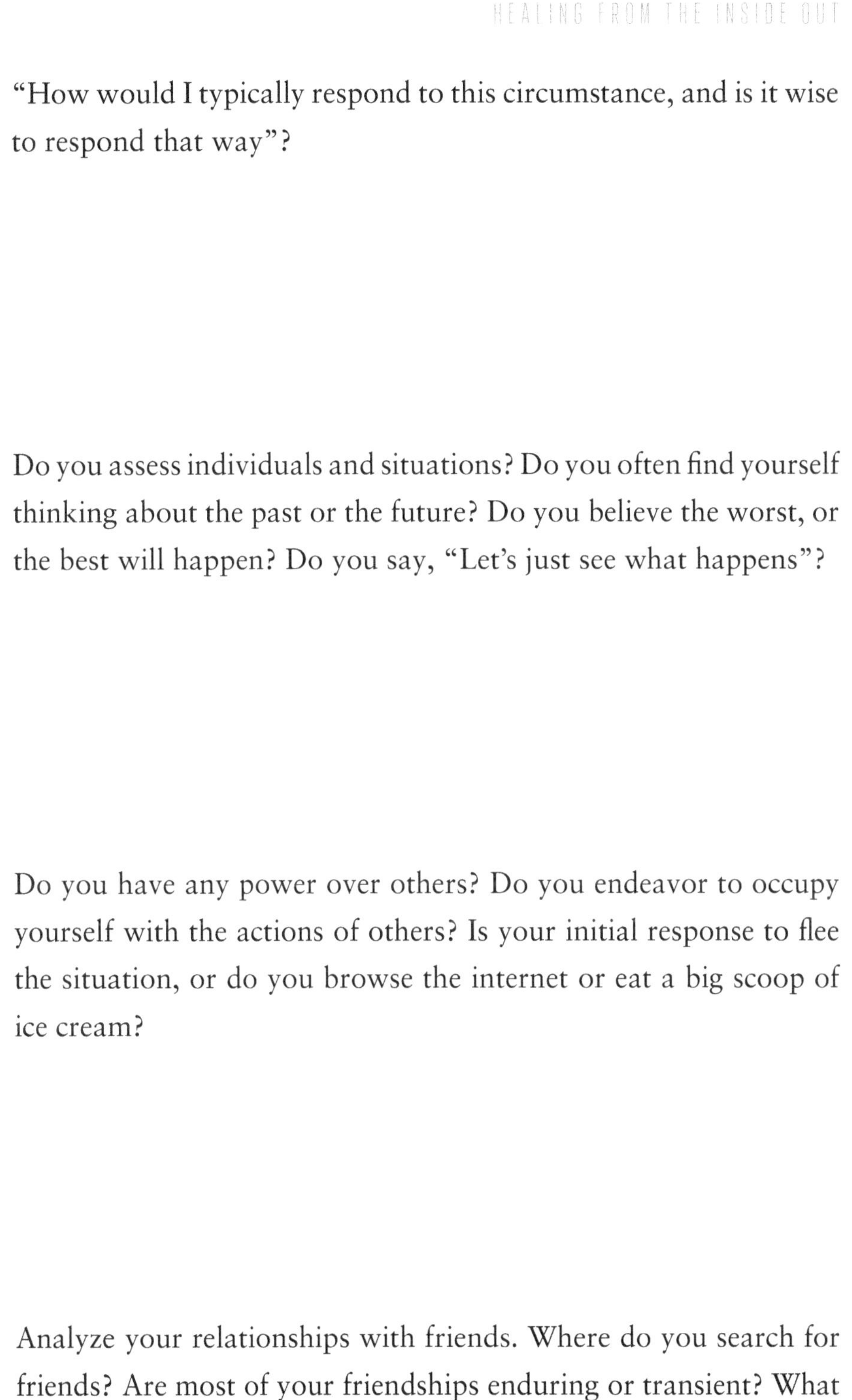

"How would I typically respond to this circumstance, and is it wise to respond that way"?

Do you assess individuals and situations? Do you often find yourself thinking about the past or the future? Do you believe the worst, or the best will happen? Do you say, "Let's just see what happens"?

Do you have any power over others? Do you endeavor to occupy yourself with the actions of others? Is your initial response to flee the situation, or do you browse the internet or eat a big scoop of ice cream?

Analyze your relationships with friends. Where do you search for friends? Are most of your friendships enduring or transient? What is the fundamental cause of your friendships breaking up? Which characters are you more interested in as friends? What kind of people should you avoid?

Look at those you are closest to. Do the people you've spoken to exhibit any patterns? What negative characteristics do they all share? What makes you believe that you were drawn to those people?

What were the weaknesses you have in your relationships? Are you a complainer, jealous, too busy with work, or unable to express your needs? Consider your role in the breakdown of your relationships if need be.

Have you modified how you behave in relationships, or do you keep making the same mistakes repeatedly?

Write in your journal. The best way to discover your identity is to record your ideas, feelings, and experiences daily. It's crucial to capture the moment in writing while it's still recent in your mem-ory because our memories of the past are frequently incomplete. Include both the day's highs and lows.

Note how well you ate and slept as well. There may be some ben-eficial information there.

Make it a habit to spend at least 15 minutes writing in your jour-nal daily. You will see trends and discover numerous things about yourself. Do you journal regularly? How will you make journaling a positive part of your daily routine?

Create a manifesto of your own. After giving it some thought, write out your perspective on life, goals, and ambitions. You could be surprised by what you write. It is an excellent start to understanding who you are and what you believe when you take this initial step.

Generate a list of your strengths and weaknesses. How did you learn? Are you certain? Avoid making rash decisions. Although you may have always believed yourself to be a hard worker, are you? To whom are you drawing analogies? Give yourself proof before you do anything.

What would people think of you? Consider the feedback from your coworkers, partner, kids, friends, and family. What do they believe you could improve on? Then ask them a question to see how accurate you are. Do you comprehend how others see you? Check your perceptual capacity.

Practice meditation. The basic purpose of meditation is to increase awareness of the present moment and of oneself. Meditation can help you become more self-aware.

- Maintain a daily meditation practice. The rest of the day should be spent being mindful of your surroundings, other people, and yourself. Increasing your level of self-awareness is as simple as paying attention.

- Ask yourself questions all day long. "What am I trying to accomplish?" What emotions am I experiencing right now, and why? "What are the emotions of those around me?"

Understanding oneself is maybe the most critical component in becoming and living authentically. The following section will guide you through considering your own identity. Observing your feelings for the rest of the day would be best. Do you observe patterns developing in similar situations?

How Do You Feel? Thoughts on Personal Identity

You have made some progress in understanding who you are because of this approach. Your identity influences everything you do and tells people a lot about you. Your thoughts and emotions comprise only a tiny portion of your identity. Let's look at a few other elements that contribute to your distinct identity:

1. Your identity significantly impacts your choices and how you interact with others.

2. Your mind, body, and behaviors will become more closely linked by meditating on who you are. You might develop a better grasp of your current situation and future goals.

3. Although there are numerous psychological views on identity, including how it arises and how it persists, consider these five essential characteristics of your identity:

- **Your family genealogy.** Strong influences on the formation of your personal identity include where you were raised, your childhood friends, and the experiences you had as you developed from an infant to your early adult years. Proverbs like "You can take the girl out of the city, but you can't take the city out of the girl" (Kidd & Davidson, 2007) come to mind. In essence, who you are is strongly influenced by your upbringing. Your past does not, however, have to be the last word on who you are right now. You may always decide to become the person you want to be, which is excellent news.

- **Your closest friends and family members** greatly influence who you are now. Your friends are probably interested in the same subjects that you find fascinating. For example, you and a few of your buddies may enjoy playing volleyball. Like some of your closest friends, you enjoy working out and are somewhat of a health nut. We are drawn to people like us even though you might associate "cliques" with your teenage years. Like the previous point, you can be selective about who you hang out with. If you want to be successful, choose to associate with successful people in both their personal and professional lives. Even though we acquaint success with finances, try leaving a person's wealth, or lack thereof, out of the equation.

- **Your physical characteristics.** The clothes you choose, your hairstyle, and how you conduct yourself physically all significantly define your identity. People may form an impression of who you are based on how you physically appear, even though there are other crucial parts of who you are besides how you appear.

- **Your opinions about you,** including your thoughts and beliefs. Your self-image is based on how you see yourself as a person. A big part of creating your identity is what you believe to be true about yourself. For instance, if you believe these things about yourself, you might accidentally tell people you are overweight and unattractive. However, if you think of yourself as someone who works hard to succeed in her field and is willing to sacrifice to acquire something, people will see you in a more favor-able light. Major components of your real identity include how you feel, think, and what you believe about yourself.

Make it a point to consider what makes you different from other people. Recognize that your identity is a complex synthesis of your history, affiliations, and self-perceived values and viewpoints. Who you are is shown by your external look. Realize how much control you have over the identity you portray to others. As you work to improve your authenticity, remain true to who you are. Even though the negative influences from your past continue to limit you now, you can still learn to let go of them.

The following section talks about your past and how remembering significant events in your life might help you better understand who you are right now. Write down the names of your top three buddies. What impact do these friends have on who you are?

Discovering Your Personal Set of Values

So far in this workbook, we've guided you toward realizing who you are. To better understand who you are, get in touch with your own set of values. It's simple to get distracted by other people's ideals and claim they are your own because of specific circumstances. You must have your own set of morals and values if you want to be able to stand by your convictions.

Simply said, your values determine the most important things to you. It's a strong belief in the principles you uphold. You can live authentically while pursuing your priorities if you know your principles.

Expanding Your Mind Through Visualizations

Finding your ideals can be done by developing a future vision. Consider several facets of your life for a while. What do you hope to achieve as you become older? What do you believe to be most crucial? What are your life objectives? These questions will help you identify your values. For example, if you want to spend valuable time with your grandchildren when you age, having a strong sense of family is one of your core beliefs.

You can have multiple values in life; you must decide which one matters most. By doing this, you may rest easy knowing that you have taken care of the things that matter most in your life at the end of each day.

Popular Values

Many people think that certain ideals are essential. Because they are a part of your core values, they may also become necessary to you. When deciding on your values, you might find the following principles helpful:

Practical. Do you depend on adrenaline? If something seems to become too routine, do you finally get bored? If so, you have a drive for exploration and would be most content trying out brand-new activities and unique approaches to your daily activities.

Communication. When you respect relationships, all your relationships, not just romantic ones, matter. It might be with any family member or friend if you value sincere relationships. This suggests that you see your relationships with family and friends as one of the most essential parts of life.

The spiritual. If you identify with a particular religion or spiritual practice, its tenets are generally highly significant to you. You might experience greater fulfillment if you spend time learning and engaging in your spiritual pursuits.

Uniqueness. Though it has many positive effects on the world, not everyone regards creativity as a fundamental trait. If you enjoy discovering new things and creating new things, it can be one of your values. Be creative while writing, listening to music, or producing something you like.

They are establishing an enduring legacy. Most people will assert that they ultimately hope to have positive memories of them. If that is one of your core principles, there are numerous ways to leave your mark on the world. Volunteering, presenting a novel idea to advance society, having a beneficial impact on others, and many more activities are examples of ways to serve others.

Finding what makes you happy is all you need to do to understand your values. Then consider why you enjoy those things. Your essential principles will become clear as you find the solutions. If your life seems to go in the wrong direction, planning for your future can help you make sense of everything. By continuing your current course, are you assisting your future self? If the response is "no," it might be time to consider choosing a different path under your underlying beliefs. When you do, you will probably find happiness on that road!

Your fundamental values are strongly tied to the things and pursuits you are enthusiastic about. What three things make you the happiest? Consider why these things bring you joy. You will probably discover some fundamental principles in your response!

Self-Reflection Questions:

Why is self-awareness necessary for living an authentic life?

Do I feel like I've ever had self-awareness before? How might knowing myself better benefit me?

How has my upbringing influenced my beliefs today? How does that impact my morals?

Which memories from my early years do I wish to keep with me in the future? Which memories do I want to let go of?

What can my friends teach me about myself?

What are my interests? How can I organize my life such that more of my routine activities align with my interests?

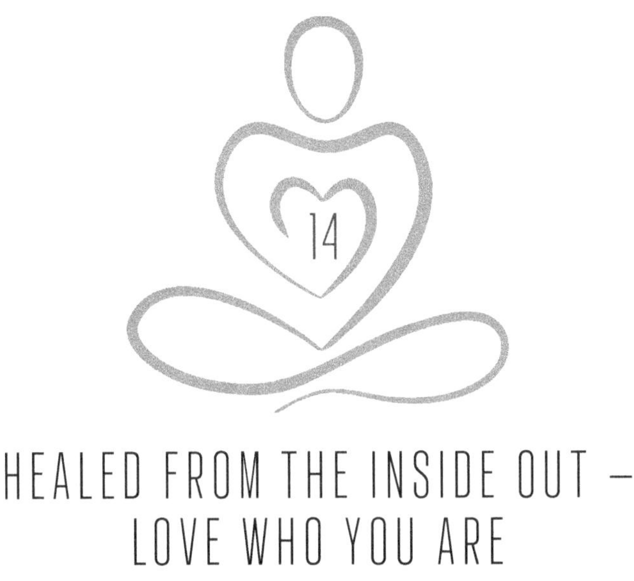

HEALED FROM THE INSIDE OUT – LOVE WHO YOU ARE

Loving Your Physical Self: Looking After Your Body

Your physical well-being and appearance reveal a lot about how you view yourself. Do you attempt to look after your body each day? When was the last time you improved how you looked? Do you regularly see your doctor and follow the instructions on your prescriptions?

We hope that each of these gets a resounding "Yes!" You try to change your poor behaviors daily if you seek personal growth and recovery. By adopting the following measures to look after your physical body, you can practice self-love:

1. Give your appearance more attention. Many of us could easily spend a few more minutes getting ready in the shower, shaving, applying cosmetics, or curling our hair.

   - Do you frequently consider the condition of your skin? Or do you waste your precious time criticizing your appearance when you stand in front of the mirror? Instead of condemning yourself, use that time to improve yourself if that is what you feel is necessary.

   - If you want to demonstrate to the world that you love yourself, put more care into your physical appearance. Take pride in who you are and how you look. You and others will both appreciate your efforts.

2. Change something. Do something different with your appearance from time to time.

   - For example, examine your appearance after shaving off your mustache or beard.

   - Get a haircut and style it like the sassy hairstyle in the saved image.

   - Make a hair color change.

   - Consider experimenting with a new look.

   - You can even change the makeup on your eyes. There are several video lessons on YouTube for various appearances.

By changing your appearance, you demonstrate your willingness to put in the time and effort required to try something new. It is also energizing. Trying it for a day or a week might give your life fresh energy, even if you decide not to keep up your new appearance.

3. Invest your energy in yourself. Realizing that you are worthy of your energy is crucial in learning to love yourself. Even if it's only ten minutes a day, focusing on something only for you sends the message that you are worthwhile.

    - Having a partner and a family can significantly sap your energy. It demonstrates that you care about yourself as much as you do for your family when you save at least some energy for yourself.

4. Take note of your bodily "pluses." With honesty, look at yourself in the mirror. Instead of focusing on what you would change, emphasize what you value. Perhaps it's your handsomely chiseled jawline or the smile in your eyes. Recognize the physical achievements in which you take pride. You can have long legs or a strong core. Perhaps you take pride in the curves of your waist or the appearance of your six-pack.

    - Give yourself plenty of time to do a physical inventory to discover attributes you should value in yourself. Think about improving your best traits to feel even better. As you become more aware of and develop positive physical characteristics, you will start to accept yourself and be well on your way to liking yourself.

5. Get more snooze time. You almost likely don't get enough sleep if you're not one of the fortunate few. To show yourself, love, sleep seven to eight hours every night.

  • Recognize that your top priorities for you are relaxing and getting enough sleep. Additionally, obtaining more sleep will increase your energy, which relates to point #3 above. Additionally, it allows you to love and inspire your family and yourself even more.

6. Be more upbeat. Try a fresh color on the off chance it may make you smile. Even something as simple as updating your wardrobe demonstrates your importance as a person. Break into a new color scheme to show you're open to experimenting with innovative ideas, whether a blazer in that current dark teal tone or a fashionable pattern shirt.

7. Consider the needs of your body. Perhaps this is the first time you have honestly thought about the types of nutrients your body genuinely needs. If you have any questions, talk to a dietitian. Paying for one or two doctor appointments will allow you to learn what your body requires to be as healthy as possible.

- If you already know what your physical self needs, use that knowledge. Donate the nutrition your body requires. Putting your body first is a lovely and profound way to express your love for yourself.

8. Give regular attention to your physical body. If your doctor allows it, try to exercise 3-5 days a week. Your body will feel better and better. Learn about the structure and purpose of your muscles, the range of motion in your limbs, and the stability of your body's core by taking some time.

    - No matter what physical activity you pick, such as calisthenics, yoga, weightlifting, or jogging, try to increase your physical performance. Start a triathlon training regimen or try learning how to dance. You will be pleasantly surprised by the pride, confidence, and care you experience for yourself when you consistently think about your physical body.

9. Recognize the good things your body accomplishes for you. Being aware of what your body is capable of is one aspect of loving yourself. Your body gives you the energy, movement, and manual dexterity you possess. It sustains you during a difficult day.

    - Every day, you can withstand much pressure on your physical self. Develop thankfulness for the near everything your body does to meet your needs. Respect your body.

10. Demonstrate a dedication to self-love. Be dedicated to living a life of unconditional acceptance of oneself. An excellent reflection of your self-esteem is how effectively you tend to your physical requirements. Commit to caring for yourself.

Taking care of your body is one of the best ways to show how much you value yourself. Fortunately, there are various ways to express your body's love. Even if you do just one thing every day, it will make you feel better. In your journal, make a list of everything positive that you can conceive about your body. Reflect on these positive traits. Feel grateful that you have them because not everyone does! Listed below is what I consider positive about my body and why I am thankful to have it:

Feeding Your Mind, Loving Your Intellectual Self

Besides loving your body and emotions, loving oneself means regularly stretching your mind. Here are some viable strategies for practicing self-love while mentally stimulating yourself.

1. Fulfill a long-held desire. In high school, did you have a strong interest in painting? Have you ever wished you could once more use a paintbrush? The time to act is right now. Researching a brand-new or popular topic may seem like a lovely pleasure. You have the right to nourish your mind; a wealth of fascinating material is available online. Start a search on a subject that interests you.

2. List the essential things in your life. What's important to you? Next, list your life goals in writing. What do you honestly hope to accomplish in life? Note how you spend most of your time. Your list should contain closely related items.

For instance,

- …have you always wanted to go to college? Do you currently dedicate most of your time to achieving that long-term goal?

- ...do you take action and obtain the additional training you require to succeed at work?

- ...if you dream of traveling, do you actively pursue it daily? Your intellect will be stimulated if you try to fulfill your deepest goals.

3. When you concentrate your time and thoughts on reaching your goals, your mind will be at its healthiest and happiest. Working in this manner also shows that you appreciate yourself enough to set your priorities straight.

4. Develop your aspirations and passions. Ask yourself and note, "What do I genuinely care about?" then investigate that subject. Utilize it. Look at it. Embrace it. If a thought, a topic, or an endeavor inspires you, go for it. Make every effort to achieve your heart's desires once you know them.

Keep up the everyday pursuit of your life's passions and aspirations. Working hard to get what you truly want is the best way to show yourself, love. Verify that you have a real life filled with real people. If you love yourself, you will have close friends and family with whom you regularly spend time. For example, spend this time "in person" with your loved ones rather than chatting with their Facebook profiles.

When you connect with people in the real world, you have a variety of possibilities to maintain your mental acuity. You will participate in exciting discussions, gain knowledge of current affairs, and have a forum to establish and express your perspectives and unique ideas.

Avoid acting in a certain way simply because "it's always been that way." Know and connect to your consciousness. Contemplate your actions before you take them. Living consciously shows that you are concerned about your life and use your ideas to deliberate your steps. When deciding with intention, you weigh all their possible outcomes. Knowing the value of time, you intelligently devote your 24-hour days to the most important pursuits. That embodies true self-love.

Make a list of your accomplishments. Make a list of your distinctive traits. Next, grab a piece of paper. To the center, draw a line. Note what is working to the left. On the right side, list the things that don't work. Decisions about the items you want to change can be made later. After that, use them. You can determine what your "thinking self" needs by engaging in this activity. By deciding what you must accomplish to develop and be intellectually challenged, you may know you are worth the time and effort to be happy. My distinctive traits are:

These are the things in my life that are working:

These are the things in my life that are not working:

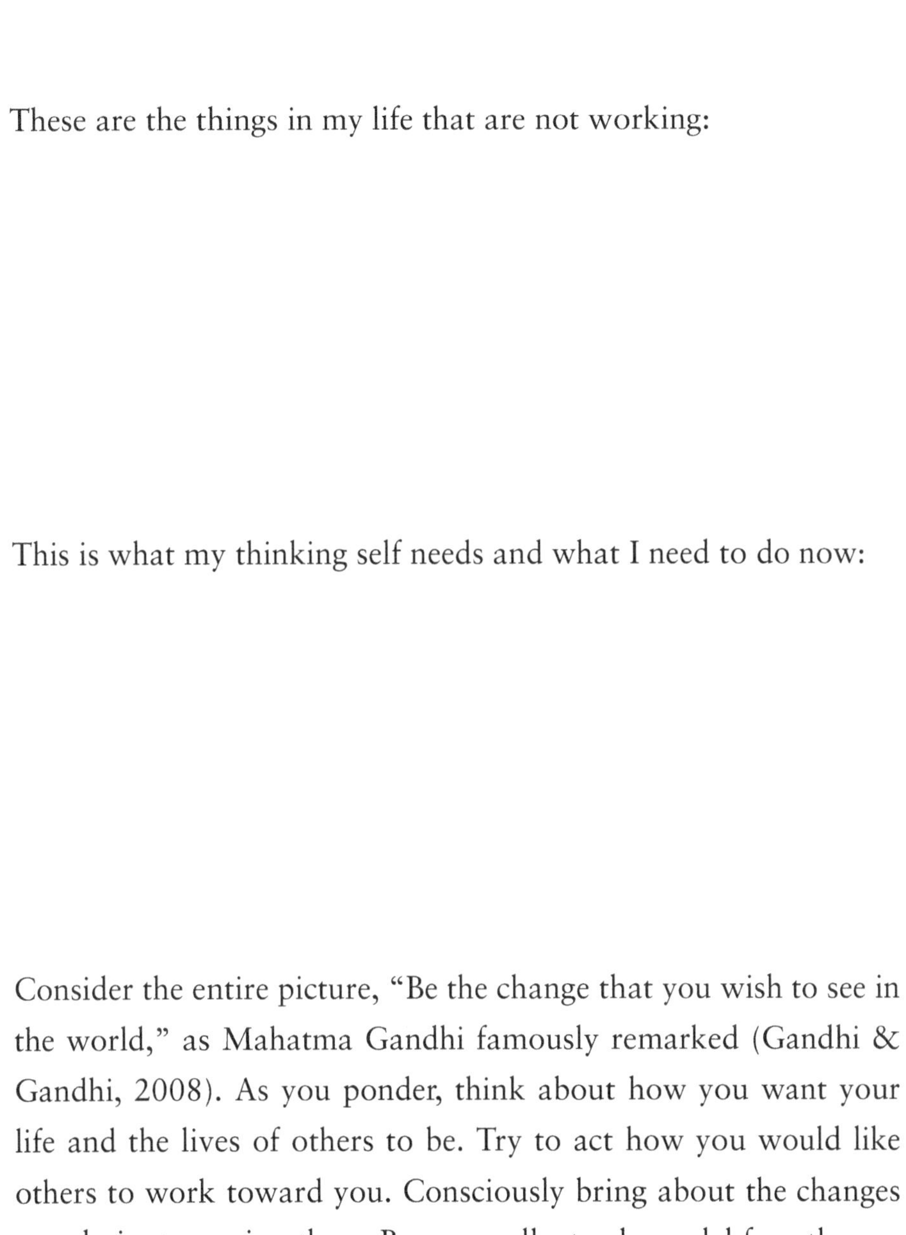

This is what my thinking self needs and what I need to do now:

Consider the entire picture, "Be the change that you wish to see in the world," as Mahatma Gandhi famously remarked (Gandhi & Gandhi, 2008). As you ponder, think about how you want your life and the lives of others to be. Try to act how you would like others to work toward you. Consciously bring about the changes you desire to see in others. Be an excellent role model for others.

- You might be perplexed about how this can be referred to as self-love, given that these actions appear so centered on affecting other people. But how can you feel bad about yourself when dedicated to improving the world?

It would be best if you affirmed your worth. Realize that everyone, including yourself, deserves to love you. Get your mind ready to embrace the love you will get from both you and other people. Recognize that you deserve every bit of love you give to yourself. If you approach life from the appropriate angle, your alternatives are limitless.

- Working on your self-confidence will open additional opportunities for self-acceptance and self-love in other areas. When you believe in your ability to make an effort, liking yourself will come much more naturally.

Find your strength. Once you understand that you have control over your thinking, you'll be free to lead the life you want. Put another way; you'll be able to use your power better.

- Discovering your power is strongly related to incorporating knowledge into your daily life. Getting more knowledge offers you more control.

Self-love entails seeking, discovering, and engaging in mental stimulation. You research issues that interest you, keep friendships with genuine people, live intentionally every day, think about the broader picture, and discover your power. You may show yourself love, by providing your mind with stimulating thoughts, ideas, and activities. You'll soon find methods to help you love your spiritual self. As stated previously, think twice before acting a certain way merely because "it's always been this way." Become aware of yourself. Do you have anything you would like to change? Is there something you want to try your way?

Here are the things I would like to change about either myself personally or my life in general, etc.:

Loving Your Spiritual Self: Caring for Your Soul

Genuine joy must be allowed to enter your spirit if you want to adore yourself fully. Allow yourself time to concentrate on your interests. Think about occasionally making minor adjustments to your home, putting away your technology regularly, and engaging in other fun and exciting activities. What strategies can help you get inspired to come up with even more original ways to demonstrate your self-care?

Listed below are some ideas to get motivated; they will help you think of even more creative methods to show that you are taking care of yourself:

1. **Have a pleasant morning.** Spend a little time doing something you enjoy in the morning. Yoga for 45 minutes could be all you need to complete your day. Before the kids get up, you might want to spend 15 minutes reading your favorite book. Or perhaps just 10 minutes to meditate will give you the peaceful start to the day you need. What do you like doing in the morning?

- Gift yourself with the morning's first few minutes. Your entire day will improve, and your spirit will appreciate you taking a little "me time" just as you get up.

2. **Indulge.** Consciously reward yourself daily. You'll enjoy life more if you try to do even one thing that makes your heart sing. Take any, pleasurable, or self-indulgent action you feel like.

- You have the means to dedicate 30 to 60 minutes a day to yourself, don't you? Loving oneself comes from knowing you deserve it.

I can reward myself daily by doing one of the following actions:

3. **Make a personal space change.** Making modest but significant modifications to your home revitalizes your spirit. Renovating a beloved room in your home is the ultimate expression of "I adore myself."

    • Clearly and thoroughly clean things.

    • Exclude certain things that make you feel uncomfortable.

    • Maybe your living room's furniture should be rearranged. Try this in your favorite room, where you spend the most time if you spend little time there.

    • Paint.

Please list below the changes you want to make to your personal space. Include when you will start doing it, the date, day, time, etc. Be specific; this will make it easier for you to follow through.

4. **Play some music.** Spend at least 15 minutes each day listening to music. Today, most phones come equipped with iPods or MP3 players. What is your favorite music, and how does it make you feel?

5. **Switch off the electronics.** Turn off your computer, television, and cell phone once a week or even once a month.

   - Disconnecting from technology is a fantastic method to re-establish a connection with your soul.

   - Consider how you would manage a day using none of your gadgets. Are you planning to relax in your yard this afternoon, take a walk, or bake some bread? Possibly your father or niece will spend the day with you. You will feel energized and at peace, no matter what you decide to do with your downtime.

What do you like doing with your downtime that has nothing to do with electronics?

6. **Permit other people's love to flow through you.** It is healthy for the soul to receive kind messages from loved ones and friends. For instance, enjoy your sister's company when you go out to lunch. Enjoy the silent dialogue you share with them, or see how they smile and make eye contact.

- You can absorb the love given by being emotionally linked to your loved ones through their presence or compliments. Although it is occasionally advised against them, compliments are good for us and are delivered out of love. Accepting them is loving oneself.

What or who makes you feel truly loved? What do they do to make you feel loved?

7. **Worship.** If you love doing it, frequenting a church, temple, or another place of worship is good for your soul. If you enjoy praying at home, doing so will help you feel deeply at peace and indicate your love for yourself.

- Perhaps you are trying to find the "right" place of worship. That's also acceptable. Finding your spiritual "home" might be a fantastic journey of self-love.

People who want to worship and successfully find the place that fits them renew their souls every time they attend the services or events that are important to them.

- Practice your religion or spirituality if it has meaning for you. Many claim that participating in worship helps them feel better.

- If you do not have a spiritual "home," explore several churches or temples to see if you can discover what your soul is longing for and the missing piece of your life. You will learn much about yourself even if you do not locate a home.

What do you like doing outdoors? Plan to spend more time in nature.

8. **Be fully present in the outdoors**—attempt to appreciate nature's delights and splendors. If you have ever taken a stroll through a pine forest, you know nature's incredible spiritual power.

- Find a method to stay connected to nature, whether you don your snowshoes and stomp through mounds of lovely white snow or stroll along a sandy beach searching for seashells.

What do you like doing outdoors? Create a plan to spend more time in nature.

9. **Be courageous.** Find the part of yourself that longs for exploration and undiscovered areas. You may go on a mountain trek, participate in a sprint triathlon, or see the Egyptian pyramids. Try to find a means to satiate your adventurous spirit. You'll feel alive and loved when you do. What would you like to try, but fear keeps you from doing it?

10. **Be conscious of the passing of time.** Spend your minutes and hours doing things that demonstrate your value. Consider each moment a priceless, once-in-a-lifetime chance to follow your passions and accomplish your goals. Decide to love yourself every single minute of every single day to make each of those moments count. You can take care of your spiritual self by practicing one or more of these techniques. Everything that makes you happy ultimately shows that you love yourself.

"Your soul is all that you possess. Take it in hand and make something of it!" *(Fischer, 1915)*

By identifying your life purpose, you can take the next step to authenticity, assemble everything, and create exciting plans for your future. Think about the suggestion given by M. Fisher for identifying your life's purpose.

LIVING YOUR BEST LIFE EVER —
PUTTING IT ALL TOGETHER

The benefits of Discovering, Living,
and Loving Your Life's Purpose

As you seek authenticity and undergo internal healing, you have been studying STS, its symptoms, and how they might impact your life. You have learned to love yourself without conditions and accept who you are. This workbook's final chapter requires you to put everything together. You can traverse STS and live your best life after everything is in order

When you first get out of bed each morning, do you dread coming to work? You can even feel pressured to join something more significant" and critical. If you are unable to recognize and decode your life's mission, you may feel unsatisfied with it. Finding the purpose of your life can be an easy endeavor. Although it could take some work, the truth is already within you. It simply needs to be discovered and put to good use. What is your life's mission currently?

If you live a life in line with your values, you can greet each day with a smile, hope, and a plan. It is a means of connecting with important things outside of oneself. Everyone has a different "why." The challenge is discovering the "why" that fits your values and skills. If your life is in a rut, the first step to living passionately and contentedly is discovering your life's purpose. "To live is to experience life to the fullest, to reach out gladly and fearlessly for greater and richer experiences" (Cervic, Marcus, Buckee, & Smith, 2021).

You may think that the word "work" has a specific meaning. You might believe that only young people and the elderly enjoy happiness; everything else is challenging and uninteresting. Life can be fascinating and meaningful at any age. Realizing that you are leading the best life for you is the key to living each day to the fullest. Knowing your life's purpose has several benefits, including:

- You'll appreciate the clarity and focus. Your attention gets diverted when you aren't putting your time and energy into the things that are important to you. Making wise selections is difficult when your purpose is unclear. Life cannot be lived without meaning, direction, or focus. Life is easier when you know what you're here for.

- You'll have more pleasure in life! Life might be more joyful if you live out your mission every day. Now that your concerns and anxieties are behind you, you can relax and enjoy yourself more.

- It increases your zest for life. If you spend your time on the most important things, your passion will be released. You'll think back to your zealous youth. You can accomplish anything when you have healthy levels of motivation and an inspiring future. This lacks life without a defined purpose.

- You gain something much more significant than yourself. You'll get a reassuring sense of peaceful certainty. It's a chance to make a substantial and lasting difference.

Your life will be changed forever if you can answer the question, "What is my life's purpose?" How can you discover what your life's mission is? You will notice that there are several tactics. In the next section, you will examine the responses to some highly significant questions that could help you understand your life's purpose. Consider how finding your life's purpose might alter your circumstances. Write three ways your life will be different and more fulfilling in your journal.

Questions to Reveal the Purpose of Your Life

Without some level of self-reflection, it is impossible to discover your purpose. Asking questions leads to finding answers. You can get the answers you need by choosing the appropriate questions. It's essential to focus on your responses when you ask yourself questions. The response you gain can be relatively muted and subdued. Be open-minded. Be sure to record your answers!

Ask yourself these helpful questions:

How would you spend the one year you had left to live? We are better equipped to concentrate on the crucial issues and let the rest go when the clock is ticking. The ideas that spring to mind deserve further thought. Could you devote your entire life to one of these concepts? Reminding oneself that life is short can be beneficial.

The awareness that you have a certain amount of time can help you stop wasting it and become decisive.

How would you like others to remember you? What would you like to be said in your obituary? How would you like to be recognized by your kids, friends, and other family members?

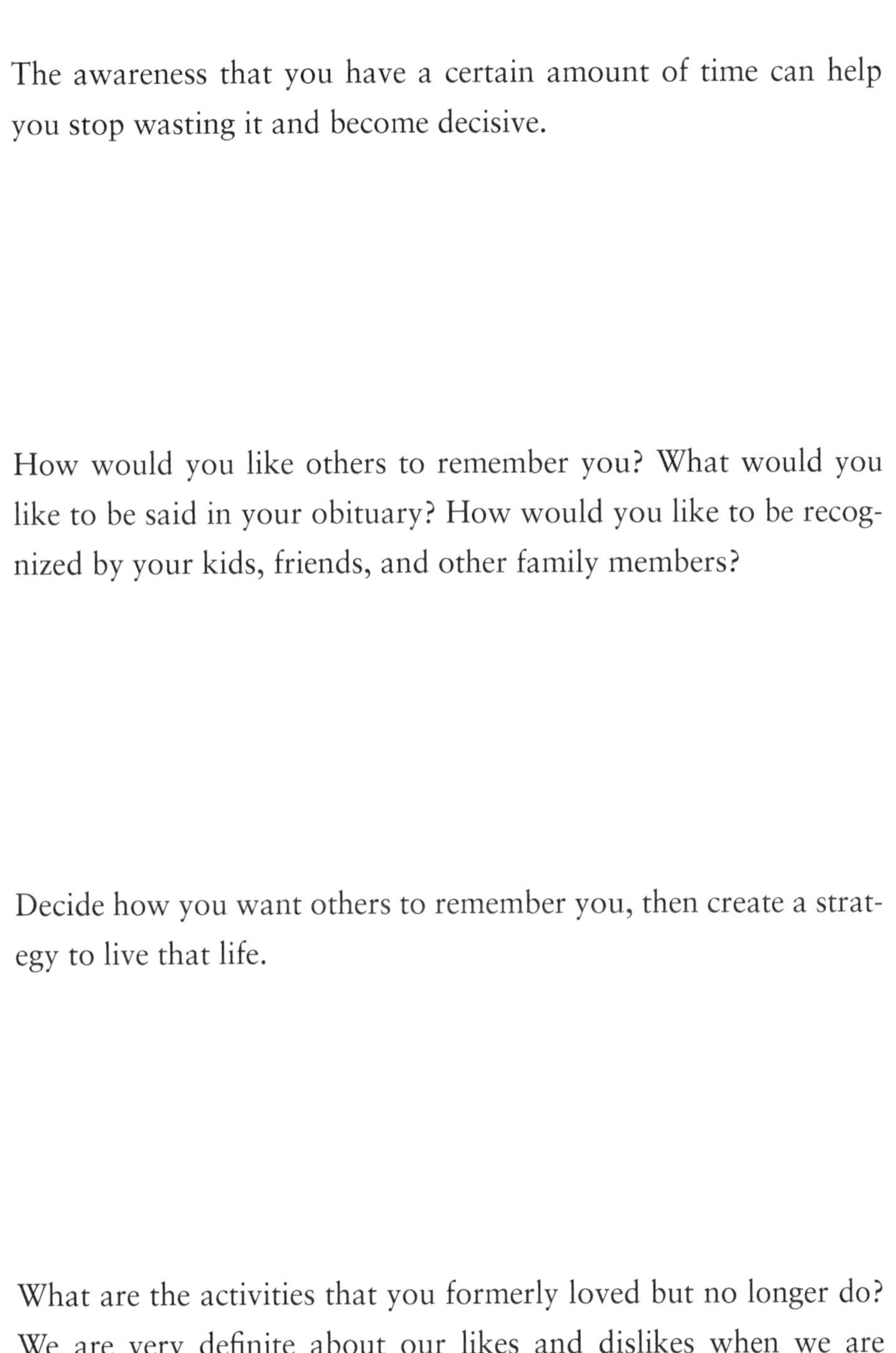

Decide how you want others to remember you, then create a strategy to live that life.

What are the activities that you formerly loved but no longer do? We are very definite about our likes and dislikes when we are young. Younger kids don't worry about other people's opinions.

When we are six years old, we only do things we enjoy. What have you discontinued over time?

As we mature into teenagers, peer pressure and the need to please others may cause us to abandon the activities we find fulfilling.

- Young adults focus too much on how realistic their decisions are. "Can I earn enough from this to live comfortably?"

You can find a method to earn a living doing what you love with a bit of thought. Life is brief. Resume the activities you formerly enjoyed and give them some ideas.

- What kind of discomfort am I capable of handling? A portion of the time, everything is terrible. The drawbacks of living your life's mission are inevitable. What are your limits?

You will be turned down at least 95% of the time if you want to be an actor, singer, writer, or artist. You will give up 80 hours a week for at least ten years if you want to start a law company.

- Would you like to teach? Can you handle the kids and parents that frequently disturb the class? Consider your decision again if you cannot handle the negative consequences of following your goal.

- What subjects and pursuits cause you to become disoriented with time? Have you ever lost yourself in a discussion or an activity where you forgot to eat or were shocked at how much time had passed?

- When you play the guitar, you could lose track of time. However, expand your line of thought. Is it music or the guitar specifically? Is it the guitar or the experience of competing with and improving yourself?

List the instances when your attention was so intense that you lost track of anything else.

Imagine if this occurrence was a part of your line of work. You would never have to "work" again!

What do you aspire to do, but avoid because of fear? Accept it. You have a fantasy about doing something, but you can't motivate yourself to do it. You could become a doctor, produce a screenplay, or scale Mount Everest.

Why have you not started by doing something? You discover that your fear frequently prevents you from trying anything new. The fear of failing, especially in front of others, is a common cause.

Remember that you must persevere through the first stage of being awful at anything to become good at it. Your first script probably won't get collected. It's likely to be terrible. But the next time will be more successful. A new skill requires practice to become proficient. In the long run, your chances of success increase the more embarrassment you can tolerate.

How can you help the planet the most? How could you best address one problem the world faces?

For true happiness, you must make a difference for someone else. None of the world's issues can be resolved by one person acting alone. Working cooperatively and creatively with others will be required of you. You might find the fulfillment you're looking for in this.

Make a list of all the ways your abilities, passions, and skills could contribute significantly to the world.

Did you answer every one of these questions? Have you recorded your responses?

How can you improve your life with the answers?

Discovering your life's meaning requires introspection. Ask yourself crucial questions, then pay attention to your responses. By responding to each of the questions listed above, you'll get the most out of this chapter. In your journal, write the questions and their responses.

Summing It All Up

Learn to prioritize the things in your life that are essential to you personally. Learn the value of being authentic with the world and the joy that comes with it. Test the advice that can help you communicate your emotions more easily. Learn to believe in your judgment. And discover how to open new doors for yourself by presenting your distinctive traits and viewpoints with pride rather than following the crowd.

With a glimpse of your exciting future, your road to healing from the inside out, becoming your authentic self, and living your best life is much closer, despite STS. To set goals based on your desires, follow the steps. Create a bucket list. Create a strategy considering all you've learned about yourself in each distinct life category, including your ideal home, profession, relationships, and other interests.

It has been a pleasure to walk you through these steps as you work through compassion fatigue and secondary traumatic stress while finding authenticity and living your most extraordinary life ever! We wish only the best for you as you proceed and enjoy the benefits of living a genuine life. What are your final thoughts? Please write them down and save this workbook with all your input. Take it out and read it whenever you think it can be helpful. Update your answers to the various questions as changes in your life evolve. You may be surprised at how much closer you have come to your authenticity.

ABOUT THE AUTHOR

Deb Alverson was born and raised in Brooklyn, N, Y. She experienced early childhood depression and trauma and became interested in trauma healing at the age of 12. Deb has earned a Bachelor of Science Degree in Human Development and holds two master's Degrees, one in Educational Counseling and another in Educational Administration.

Deb became an expert in healing from Compassion Fatigue, Secondary Traumatic Stress, and Vicarious Trauma through her own experiences, living in and serving recipients in a community in Utah which has facetiously been titled "The Armpit of Utah," and in Bush, Alaska serving the Alaska Native Community. Her level of expertise has led to her conducting research, delivery of many professional development presentations, application of research to practice, and delivery of hands-on classroom training.

Deb Alverson lives in the Mid-Hudson Valley with her husband, Jim, Border Collie, Mia, and Tuxedo Cat, Socks. She enjoys spending quality time with her four sons and two granddaughters.

REFERENCES

Banks, J. (2022). I Love Me More: How to Find Happiness and Success Through Self-love. Greenleaf Book Group.

Blanchard, K., & Broadwell, R. (2021). Servant leadership in action: How you can achieve great relationships and results. Berrett-Koehler Publishers, Inc..

Burger, W. E. (1970). No man is an island. ABAJ, 56, 325.

Cevik, M., Marcus, J. L., Buckee, C., & Smith, T. C. (2021). Severe acute respiratory syndrome coronavirus 2 (SARS-CoV-2) transmission dynamics should inform policy. Clinical Infectious Diseases, 73(Supplement_2), S170-S176.

Chan, W. T. (2015). The Way of Lao Tzu. Ravenio Books.

Chandrasekhar, S. S. (2021). Building the Future, We Wish to See. Otolaryngologic Clinics of North America, 54(4), xvii-xix.

Children's exposure to violence: A comprehensive national survey. (n.d.). Retrieved March 1, 2023, from https://www.ojp.gov/pdffiles1/ojjdp/227744.pdf

Dixon-Woods, M., Campbell, A., Martin, G., Willars, J., Tarrant, C., Aveling, E. L., Sutcliffe, K., Clements, J., Carlstrom, M. & Pronovost, P. (2019). Improving employee voice about transgressive or disruptive behavior: a case study. Academic Medicine, 94(4), 579.

Encarnación-Pinedo, E. (2022). Ethnicity and Gender in the Beat Generation: Jack Kerouac and the Other Woman. International Journal of English Studies, 22(1), 1-21.

Feldman, R. (2020). What is resilience: an affiliative neuroscience approach. World Psychiatry, 19(2), 132-150.

Fischer, M. H. (1915). Oedema and nephritis. J. Wiley.

Fogg, B. J. (2019). Tiny habits: The small changes that change everything. Eamon Dolan Books.

Gandhi, M., & Gandhi, M. K. (2008). The essential writings. Oxford University Press.

Garrett, H. (2022). The Intensity of the Inevitable: The Motif of Tension in Ernest Hemingway's in Our Time. Johns Hopkins University, 3(1).

Gibran, K. (2022). Sand and foam. Open Road Media.

Gilbert, A. (2021). Kindness now: A 28-day guide to living with authenticity, intention, and compassion. Shambhala Publications.

Harris, K. I. (2019). Fred rogers and children's spirituality: Valuing the uniqueness of others and caring for others. International Journal of Children's Spirituality, 24(2), 140-154.

Hay, L. L., & Kessler, D. (2015). You Can Heal Your Heart: Finding Peace After a Breakup, Divorce, Or Death. Hay House, Inc.

Jacobs, I., Charmillot, M., Martin Soelch, C., & Horsch, A. (2019). Validity, reliability, and factor structure of the secondary traumatic stress scale-French version. Frontiers in psychiatry, 10, 191.

Kennedy, B. (2020). A 21st century appreciation for: Quality, excellence and complex human adaptive systems. The TQM Journal, 32(1), 2-20.

Kennedy, J. R. (2022). No more secrets (Vol. 37). UnderMill Press.

Kheybari, S., Naji, S. A., Rezaie, F. M., & Salehpour, R. (2019). ABC classification according to Pareto's principle: a hybrid methodology. Opsearch, 56, 539-562.

Kidd, S. A., & Davidson, L. (2007). "You have to adapt because you have no other choice": The stories of strength and resilience of 208 homeless youth in New York City and Toronto. Journal of community psychology, 35(2), 219-238.

Kübler-Ross, E. (2014). The AZ of death and dying: Social, medical, and cultural aspects. The AZ of Death and Dying: Social, Medical, and Cultural Aspects, 286.

Leigh, A. (2021). What's the Worst that Could Happen? Existential Risk and Extreme Politics. MIT Press.

Matthews, A. (1997). Follow your heart: Finding purpose in your life and work. Seashell Publishers.

Miaw, D. (2019). Dream BIG. The Flutist Quarterly, 44(3), 48-49.

Morin, A. (2011). Self‐awareness part 1: Definition, measures, effects, functions, and antecedents. Social and personality psychology compass, 5(10), 807-823.

Organizational and individual stress management. SAMHSA. (n.d.). Retrieved March 1, 2023, from https://www.samhsa.gov/dtac/disaster-response-template-toolkit/organizational-individual-stress-management

Osteen, J. (2021). Peaceful on Purpose: The Power to Remain Calm, Strong, and Confident in Every Season. FaithWords:Chicago

Rauvola, R. S., Vega, D. M., & Lavigne, K. N. (2019). Compassion fatigue, secondary traumatic stress, and vicarious traumatization: A qualitative review and research agenda. Occupational Health Science, 3, 297-336.

Rizvi, T. (2022). 2022 Erma Bombeck Writers' Workshop Program.

Russ-Eft, D. F., Bober, M. J., De La Teja, I., Foxon, M., & Koszalka, T. A. (2008). Evaluator competencies: Standards for the practice of evaluation in organizations (Vol. 22). John Wiley & Sons.

Samhsa - Substance Abuse and Mental Health Services Administration. (n.d.). Retrieved March 1, 2023, from https://www.samhsa.gov/sites/default/files/brief_report_natl_childrens_mh_awareness_day.pdf

Springer, C. (2021). The Postcolonial Rebel. In James Dean Transfigured (pp. 134-163). University of Texas Press.

Thurman, H. (1981). With head and heart: The autobiography of Howard Thurman. Houghton Mifflin Harcourt.

Ting, L., Jacobson, J. M., Sanders, S., Bride, B. E., & Harrington, D. (2012). The secondary traumatic stress scale (STSS): Confirmatory factor analyses with a national sample of mental health social workers. In Approaches to Measuring Human Behavior in the Social Environment (pp. 177-194). Routledge.

Williams, K. (2020). What imaginative literature can teach us about bullying. International journal of bullying prevention, 2(3), 170-179.

Year, H. N. Merrimac State School Newsletter. Sage, 100, 6C.